AGRICULTURAL GROWTH AND NON-AGRICULTURAL GROWTH

Dynamics of National Development

Agricultural Growth and Non-Agricultural Growth

DYNAMICS OF NATIONAL DEVELOPMENT

Dr. T.K. METI
M. A., Ph. D.

GIAN PUBLISHING HOUSE
NEW DELHI-110002

Gian Publishing House
4348 Madan Mohan Street
4-C Ansari Road, Daryaganj
New Delhi-11002

To
My Mother
Shrimati Lingamma Karabasappa Meti

ISBN-81-212-0272-8

Printed in India

Published by Mrs. Gayatri Garg for Gian Publishing House, New Delhi-110002
Printed by Amar Composing Agency, Delhi-32

Foreword

This slim volume is a study of the interaction between agricultural growth and non-agricultural growth with reference to India. The author, Dr. T.K. Meti, has put in a considerable amount of thinking and hard work in the preparation of this study.

We have been accustomed so much in the past with the controversy in regard to priorities between these two areas and whether industrial development should precede agricultural development. The general tendency in many developing countries has always been to emphasise on industrial development as we see in the developed countries and their prosperity due largely to the development of their industrial sector. In actual fact, there can be no question of industrial development unless there is agricultural development and agricultural development in turn depends upon industrial development. When agriculture was in a primitive stage, it was just a producer who supplied for the consumption of the urban sector and generally did not derive any advantage of its own productive system. With modernisation, however, agricultural sector has began to use a large volume of industrial inputs and this tendency has been growing over the time. Not only that, even some of agricultural products are becoming industrialised and synthetic substitutes are taking place of earth-grown raw materials. With the modernisation of agriculture, services also play an important part in the development of agriculture. More recently, the importance given to food processing industries has brought in an element of industrialisation into modern agriculture. In fact, therefore, one can see that with growth and development it is not only industry that gets developed but agriculture also gets modernised and acquires industrial characteristics and, similarly, services not only are production oriented and consumption-oriented, but also deals with repairs and maintenance of the machinery, equipment, etc. going into agricultural and industrial production,

Thus, the whole three sectoral division of the national product becomes an integrated affair and there can be no major development in other sectors.

One thing is clear, however, that agriculture cannot be neglected and industrial growth given primary importance, for not only it provides raw materials for the industry but also produces surplus food for consumption by industrial producers. Therefore, the emphasis placed on agrtcultural development by development economists is perfectly sound and applies also to Indian conditions.

One more relevent point in development which is becoming important in recent years is the influence of environment on production and the recognition that environmental and ecological considerations should be taken into account in any scheme for promoting industrial or agricultural or service development.

Dr. Meti's study is quite interesting and throws some light on the points mentioned above as also discusses the relative role of these three sectors in international trade and the growing importance of service sector in international trade, besides industrial and agricultural production. It brings in a small compass some of the vital considerations affecting the relationship between the different sectors of the economy, and should be welcomed by readers in the theme of economic development.

Prof. V.K.R.V. RAO

Preface

Several changes have been taking place all over the globe in a number of parameters of development and progress for over the last four decades. Interactions and interrelationships among these different variables need to be studied for sake of synchronisation and coordination just to avoid their adverse conflicts that may retard the overall growth process. Besides balance between agriculture and industry which has to be equitable in its operations not only across national boundaries but also between them, the balance between economic growth that includes all the sectors, and the environmental soundness that covers them all, has not only to be implemented all over the world but also in between themselves. Indian economic development in particular is also not an exception to these observations.

I took a lot of interest in developing my views on these issues as it was supposed to be the need of the hour when India experienced planning lessons for the last four decades and when the world witnessed numerous vicissitudes and vibrations in its structure and nature especially after the World War II. The result of my thinking, reading and reference in this perspective has been the present work, namely, Agricultural Growth and Non-Agricultural Growth : Dynamics of National Development. Micro and Macro approaches towards understanding of development process and focussing on interactions through the analysis of inter-sectoral linkages, inter-industry dependence, international trade composition of agricultural produce and non-agricultural goods and products, environmental sustenance, etc. have been the highlights of the present study. I am sure that this study does cater to the needs of student community of Economics discipline, professors and teachers of Economics, research students and policy makers at both State and National levels.

In the pursuit and completion of my work, I have to acknowledge with gratitude the help and cooperation that I received from a number of persons, institutions and organisations. Dr. V.K.R.V. Rao, an eminent and world renowned economist who is now a National Professor of Economics in India has taken lot of pains in preparing 'Foreword' to my book. In spite of his tender health, he made it a point to respond to my request in this context. I, therefore, owe a great deal of gratitude to him. The present study took birth in the premises of Karnatak University, especially as a part of research studies in the Department of Studies in Economics. Though it is an individual research, I should not forget all sorts of facilities provided by the University in the form of library references, and other congenial atmosphere for such studies. I thank the Karnatak University and my colleagues in the Department of Studies in Economics for their cooperation. My thanks also go to Mr. S.L. Bilagi who has typed my manuscript neatly. I do keep on record direct and indirect encouragement that I received from my wife Susheela and sons as well as daughters in keeping me undisturbed while I was at desk for preparing the present work. So far as publication of the study is concerned, M/s Gian Publishing House, New Delhi came with encouraging response. Mr. B.P. Garg, Chief Executive and Mr. A.P.S. Chauhan, Managing Editor, Gain Publishing House have extended their cooperation in getting the present study published. I thank them sincerely.

(T.K. METI)

Professor & Chairman
Department of Studies in Economics,
Karnatak University
DHARWAD – 580003.

Contents

1

Introduction

Economic development is a process that involves structural changes arising from action and interaction of different forces and factors that help increase the national output. "......economic development is a process......Process implies the operation of certain forces; these forces operate over the long period and embody changes in certain variables. Details of the process vary under diverse conditions in space and time. ......And the general result of the process is growth in an economy's national product—in itself a particular long-run change".[1] The main focus of development of an economy, therefore is (a) to ascertain the various components that form and influence the nature and norm of the economy, (b) to reflect how and why changes occur in such ingredients, (c) to enlist the causal relationship in between different changes, and (d) to assess how far and how long such relations result in an increase of national income and thereby per-capita income.

---

1. 'Economic Development Theory, History, Policy,' by G.M. Meier & R.E. Baldwin, 1961, p. 2.

Every economy is composed of different factors and sectors which operate and move the economy in one direction or the other. Such of them are land, capital, population, technology, organisation, institutions and cultural values. By the very nature of their operations (a process) changes creep in by the forces and policies of development. Generally these changes multiply as the time passes and go on influencing each other. The causal relationship among these changes is a governing and motive force of the development phenomenon. Since many changes are of short-period and give way to long-period changes, the development problem is to take into account the long-period changes that cause a rise in the national income. Though there happen to be some growth retarding changes, they are to be overcome in the process of development. It is therefore the concern of the development to manipulate the growth-promoting changes and forces.

The changes brought about by the development process effect an augmentation of national output, that, is in other words, national income, proper. For instance, land manifested in the national resources undergoes a change by way of intensive and extensive type of cultivation. This method of cultivation usually causes a rise in productivity that conduces capital formation by increased savings in that sector. Again as a result of capital formation, new technologies are bound to be adopted and in turn technical progress in agricultural tends to be fostered. Subsequently, more and more employment opportunities open. In the process, men behind the ploughs are induced to adjust with the changes and transform themselves to adapt to the changing circumstances. Consequently, their values and institutions undergo a change and many times the poeple bccome ready to accept and follow new values and institutions.

Capital is a very vital factor for every economic activity. It arises from autonomous and induced savings. Once it is formed, it breeds a number of stimulants that facilitate development. Autonomous savings are the resultant of increases in productivity of overall economy. Especially in respect of developing economies, due to low productivity capital deficiency is quite noticeable. Though the efforts are made by way of planning to increase productivity that generates savings, capital requirements of the development cannot be met fully without induced savings including foreign borrowings. Nevertheless, increased investment in a number of industries enhances the capital formation. Similarly, investment in physical infrastructure also reinforces capital accumulation that pushes up the development process. Further, capital formation promotes technological and technical progress which in turn increases the economic productivity. As the technical progress is a result of the entrepreneural initiatives, manpower development takes place. Thus, both physical capital and human capital are built and cause the development in expeditious manner.

Population which is one of the determinants of economic development plays a very important role. The nature of population shapes the growth process. If people are motivated, enlightened, educated and adventurous, the rate of the growth tends to be faster and higher and vice versa. Even the distribution of population according to occupations decides the norm of development. If occupational distribution is diversified and wider, the development becomes rapid and vigorous. The size of population, other features remaining constant, serves as a limiting factor. Higher and denser the population, it tends to be burdensome and vice-versa. Rate of growth of population has to be commensurate with the rate of growth of national income. If the former is higher than the latter, consequences are undesirable. The problems of unemployment, houselessness, social stresses etc. become rampant. Ii is therefore necessary that population growth has to be geared to the requirements of development. Thus, human resources development becomes inevitable.

Institutions serve both as levers and agencies of development. These institutions being political, economic and social, sway much influence. Of course, in the wake of development, some of the old institutions disappear, some others get modified and new institutions come up. Arrangement of these institutions for helping and monitoring economic development becomes imperative. It the institutions are not properly informed of their tasks and responsibilities, development tends to be slow and to a certain extent halved. "To be effective, economic institutions must be adapted to the needs and the culture of a country. The adaptation may be undertaken consciously. In the optimal case, however, institutions evolve to fit a country's economic requirements and its national character in a subtle and unconscious way......The institutions, used in a given country at a given stage of its development for production, distribution, allocation of credit, and for associating producers, consumers, and the public in the process, are most effective when they fit both the economic needs and the cultural conditions of the country".[2] Institutional reform in China in recent times is an instance and evidence in this context.

Organisation is another important factor that goads economic development. Especially in less developed countries and developing economies, it is a scarce factor. Though sometimes, organisation is considered another form and function of labour, it has a special role to play in the process of economic development. Following Harbisan [3] we propose to regard the man as an organiser and the task as organisation. It is not enough to say that growth is a function of land, capital, labour and technology. There must be some element or factor which combines these in the right proportions, sets the task, and sees to its accomplishment. According to Schumpeter, organisation is also counted to be an entrepreneurial capacity. Entrepreneurship and organisation are more or less synonyms. Again, administration is usually called organisation. Hirschman, for that matter, identifies, in another sense organisation as decision-making capacity. In his view, the scarcest talent in developing countries is decision-making. Decision making capacity grows with practice, is a learning process. If the central authorities can induce pressures for decision-making,

2. Economic Development, (International Student 2nd edition) by C.P. Kindleberger, p. 38.

3. "Entrepreneurial Organisation, as a Factor in Economic Development" Quarterly Journal of Economics, August 1956, pp. 364-379.

they will advance growth by breaking critical bottle-necks.[4] It is in this connection necessary to emphasize the human resources development. Unless the people are fashioned as human capital, the development process of the developing economies does not proceed rapidly and smoothly.

Cultural values, attitudes and social etiquettes form non-economic factors and forces that are crucially operating as conditions for economic growth. In developing economics most of which were colonies of the foreign rule, legacies of colonial government, cross-cultural conflicts, inter-cultural clashes, caste-confrontations, class-struggles etc. are found in existence. Age-old beliefs, social taboos, traditional barriers etc. do still prevail and condition the life-styles of the people of such countries. Under such circumstances, changes that are necessiated by development policies and measures meet with resistances. In order to get peoples' participation, and cooperation, proper harnessing and harmonising of cultural values and people's attitudes assume a great importance. "A progressive society inculcates attitudes and provides incentives favourable to economic growth ; a stagnant one does not."[5] Backward sloping supply curve of labour, fatalism, hoarding class-structure, belief in 'tantrik' and 'mantrik' methods, re-birth etc. are some of the growth-retarding conditions. All these inhibitious and rigidities have to be vanquished and the people have to be dynamic, adventurous, risk-bearers, and motivated for shouldering the tasks of development.

For the purposes of the present study, various forces are classified into agricultural and non-agricultural ones. In developing economies such as India, primary sector is an agricultural sector. Any movement in the direction of development generally originates in this sector or tends to bring about changes therein. Economic history of Europe, the continent which has the privilege of containing the developed

---

4. The Strategy of Economic Development, 1958, Chapt. 4.

5. Economic Development—Principles, Problems and Policies, by Benjamin Higgins, Central Book Depot, Allahabad, 1961, p. 257.

countries earlier than other continents in the world, shows that agricultural revolution preceded the industrial revolution though the latter continued to be perpetually marching ahead of agricultural progress. "——in the 1740s, an increase in farm productivity based on scientific farming, better crops' rotations, stall feeding of animals, and so on, preceded the spurt in industry known as the Industrial Revolution."[6] But the fact remains that even in developed countries in their initial stages of growth, the changes in agricultural sector proved to fore-runner of change in industrial sector. "Industrialisation has in fact depended a good deal upon transfers of "savings" (i.e. non-consumed income) from the agricultural sector to industrial investments in many countries."[7] Of course, in due course, it is the industrial changes that have dominated the process of development. However, as far as the development of developing countries is concerned, transformation of traditional agriculture appears to be prerequisite. "——a developing country, even if it trades extensively with other nations, have every reason to direct its main efforts at first to raising agricultural incomes beyond the level of demand for essentials, and to postpone to a later date the stimulation of industrial production and of services. The key to development is the growth of agricultural income, and if a country fails to achieve this before all else, the whole development process may be held back : at best growth rates will vary greatly from one part of the country to another and this is certainly not conducive to balanced growth and adds to the number of problems to be solved".[8] In the march of such development, agriculture fosters the industrial development and industrial development in turn reinforces the progress of agriculture. Though such observations are apparently

---

6. Economic Development, (2nd edition, international student edition) by C.P. Kindleberger, p. 216.

7. Agricultural Revolution and Economic Progress, by Rainer Schickele, 1969, p. 73.

8. Problems in Economic Development, edited by E.A,G. Robinson, p. 76.

available, such questions as what is the extent of mutual reinforcement ? How does it take place ? and others need to be dealt with in detail.

Generally it is noticed that for the overall growth of any country both agricultural and non-agricultural sectors together work harmoniously and complementarily. However, certain instances point out that wherever primary producing sector is dominant growth rate of such countries appear to be lower and lesser than the growth rate of other countries where industrial sector dominates. This observation perhaps has been based on an assumption that industrial concerns with capital intensive large size plants yield increasing returns than the agricultural persuits which lack in such economies. Of course, given other things constant, this observation holds good. especially when the comparison is made between developed countries and the developing countries. But it is to be mentioned here that there are some primary producing countries such as Australia, New Zealand, etc., which are considered to be among the developed nations in the world. In these countries, agriculture has been modernised and risen as much productive as industrial activities. This gives a clue to how development policy needs to be devised depending upon the peculiar features of different countries.

There is still one more notion that economic development is synonymous with industrialisation.[9] This view perhaps is based on the lessons that obtain in most of the developed countries. In these nations, it is industrial sector that goads the development process. The development is measured and understood in terms of size and number of industries that operate in the process of development. The promotion of directly productive activities that are the features of industrialization breed interdependence of industries and generate both internal and external economies. These forces enlarge the base and coverage of industrial activities which in turn promote and

9. Hollis B. Chenery "Role of Industrialization in Development Programmes" pp. 451-471, In : The Economics of Underdevelopment edited by A.N. Agarwala & S.P. Singh, 1958.

strengthen social overhead capital. Even the agricultural sector is so modernised as to be counted on par with industry. But, this view is to be totally unacceptable. To a large extent industrialization is the main indicator of development, but not the whole content of it. Economic development is resultant of actions and interactions of a number of variables of which industrialization is one. It is quite obvious tha t there are non-economic factors such as institutions, values, motivations, etc. which are subtle forces that influence economic development. In addition, there is what is known as human factors that play an important role in economic development.

The economic development is designed to bestow many benefits and facilities on people. Such issues as how the advantages and other conveniences are created in the economies ? how they are supplied to the people ? and how far the people are responding to the challenges of development ? are again matters depending on the nature and attitudes of the people. In some countries, certain sections of the people having command over the capital and entrepreneurship initiated the development and consequently many physical facilities were created for the rest of the people. This kind of development is seen in capitalistic countries. In some other countries, it is the people who organised themselves into some kind of united force to uplift themselves. There happens to be no difference between people and the government. This reminds us of the examples of Russia and China. Still there are such countries wherein the government attempts to educate and motivate the people for shouldering the tasks of development so as to improve their lot. These are the instances of most of the developing countries.

It is now openly recognised that the role of human factor is increasingly important to further the growth process. The economists such as Schultz, Denison, and Colin Clark have authoritatively proved this fact. Prof. Schultz established that the increase in productivity of the American economy in recent years owed much to the contribution of human capital, whereas Prof. Clark has ably demonstrated the crucial role of human factor in the transformation of traditional agriculture.

"And the contribution of education to American growth has been most pronounced in the more recent decades, while capital investment was more important in earlier decades."[10] Even in the very recent findings about the performance of plan programmes in most of the developing economies including India, it is found that the people's participation and involvement is very much missing so as to account for the failure in achieving the desired targets of development. Hence, the development measures in these countries are devised to tone up the motivation of people for the development purposes.

As economic development is measured, among other yardsticks, by the rate of growth of national product, it is quite interesting to note the changes in the trends of composition of national product of different countries in order to ascertain how far agricultural sector and other sectors witnessed a change in their shares in the total output of the countries. Generally, it is observed that as an economy grows, the share of agricultural sector declines and the shares of other sectors increase. This fact is illustrated by certain tendencies of both agricultural and non-agricultural sectors. The agricultural sector having certain rigidities in terms of its institutions and its inherent characteristics such as law of diminishing returns etc., appears to respond increasingly in a diminishing manner to the call of development measures. Industrial sector and service sector, on the other hand, prove to be more favourably responsive to development achievements. Relatively speaking, it is the service sector where human ingenuity plays very strategic role, will have an increasing importance in the days to some. Of course, the human element has already proved its significance in technological and entrepreneurial aspects of development. Further, its contribution seems to have an unlimited value in the future course of events that take place in the process of development.[11]

---

10. Demison, E.F., p. 601, Leading Issues in Economic Development, by Gerald, M.Meier, and see Transforming Traditional Agriculture by Colin Clark.
11. For details see "Human Capital Approach to Economic Development" by A.V. Alex, 1983.

There is still one more aspect which relates to the differing roles of these sectors. It is the composition of national and international trade consisting of imports and exports. In order to augment the welfare of people in the world, total quantum of international trade should increase. In this context, it is very essential to assess to what extent different countries on the globe contribute to the rise in the world-trade.

The components of national and international income are again other indicators of relative importance of different origins of income. It is usually believed that in most of the developing countries the agricultural sector contributes 40 to 70 per cent of the total national income while in the developed countries other sectors play a major role in this connection. Though very recently, the GNP approach towards understanding the growth rate is not much convincing, it appears to be a convenient and less complicated method. Comparative picture of the roles of different sectors in between or among a number of countries in the world is perhaps an interesting and revealing phenomenon. From this analysis, it becomes clear that a number of new economic activities emerge in the wake of economic development of each country. As is already mentioned, the development policies and programmes are thus to be chalked out to have cumulative and coordinating growth of all such sectors and economic activities.

From the foregoing paragraphs, it is very clear to understand the importance and objectives of the present study of interaction between agricultural and non-agricultural growth. Since many of the developing economies have not an integrated economic system, it is this study which helps how the integration of economic activities will have to be established. The integration process is very easily understood when interdependence and inter-sectoral linkages are assessed and quantified. Of course, the integration does not mean that each sector of an economy loses its identity. On the other hand, all the sectors that constitute an economy will be developed in their proper perspective. It is only when each sector is properly sized up that the development policies of overall development of an economy will be meaningful.

The main objectives of the study are (1) to understand the distinguishing features of agriculture, industry and service-sector for ascertaining the role of each one of them in its own perspective and framework; (2) to know the inter-sectoral linkages; (3) to highlight such interdependence with available statistics and studies even in the sphere of international trade; and (4) to suggest new policies and programmes.

Keeping in view all the above objectives, the study proceeds with an introductory chapter containing different dimensions of the study. In Chapter-2, an analysis of the role of agriculture is taken up, Chapter-3 attempts to depict the features and prospects of industrial sector. The significant traits of service-sector are analysed in Chapter-4. Chapter-5 aims at assessing the intersectoral linkages with reference to India on the basis of some studies that have been already undertaken in this connection. In Chapter-6. the place of international trade in agricultural commodities with respect to different countries in the world including India has been ascertained. The last Chapter contains certain meaningful conclusions that have bearing on future policies and programmes of development of agricultura! economy in developing countries so as to enlist its rate of growth relatively on par with the growth of non-agricultural sector.

2

Agriculture in Economic Development

Among different determinants of economic development, land is unique due to its peculiar features. Unlike other factors of production, it is limited in supply and it is heavily controlled or conditioned by climatic and weather conditions. Its fertility is, unlike age-old belief, exhaustible. Food, an outcome of land, happens to be a basic necessity of mankind to live on. Some of the natural resources, manifestations of land, are not renewable and as such they create unexpected tumults in the international scene, for instance, rationing of petroleum products in recent times. Income-elasticity of demand for food is less than one and as such higher income-growth of a nation does not serve as an incentive for increasing expansion of agricultural produce. In the absence of crop-insurance and livestock insurance, investment in agriculture appears less rewarding and is full of uncertainties and risks. Especially in most of the developing countries due to in-built rigidities and innate disincentives for agricultural persuits, technological development in agriculture is slower than in industrial sector. Above all, peasants who are operating on the land are less entrepreneurial than the industrialists. It is therefore imperative on the part of agriculture to seek external support to develop on par with industry. Besides, it is observed in many instances that the supply curve of labour in agriculture is back-ward sloping.

In spite of the above limitations of agriculture, the significance of agriculture is not to be under-rated. There are three schools of thought which have viewed agriculture in relation to other sectors of an economy and which have placed agriculture in an enviable position as compared to the other sectors such as industry and service sector. The school comprising Barker, Wilson, Barsodi, Humphries and others are said to have held an orthodox view of agricultural fundamentalism. It bears witness to a wide-spread, deep-seated, persistent conviction that agriculture is par excellence the fundamental industry, and that farmers are, in a peculiar sense and degree, of basic importance in society. The existence of human race owes much to agriculture as it provides a basic necessity i.e. food for mankind. It caters to the needs of commerce and manufacturing by supplying to them agricultural raw materials. Agricultural life is more natural than modern life which is becoming more mechanical, commercial and artificial. Many more values of life are to be learnt from the farmers residing in rural areas, such as independence, non-interference, simplicity, honesty, and straight-forward nature. It will never be possible to have a civilization wholly urban and industrial which neglects agriculture completely. These people believe that without contributions of agriculture, our civilization does not sustain itself forever.

There is another extreme school which holds modern view that prosperity of a nation depends largely on other factors than the work of those who till the soil. It is shown that in the course of development of an economy, the importance of agriculture declines. Its share in national income decreases as compared to the shares of other sectors and activities. The people depending on agriculture go on diminishing in number as urbanisation takes place. Even the employment in agriculture declines as other non-agricultural activities grow. There will be a falling ratio of agricultural population to the total population. Thus, wealth and welfare of nations depend upon many complex conditions and today agriculture is not uniquely basic. It is the industrial sector which dominates every economy in ultimate analysis and it is the urban sector which has bright future as compared to rural sector. J.S. Davis is the most popular representative of this school.

Karl Brandt, H.R. Tolley and others take a more balanced view. After considering eastern and western countries, agricultural and industrial countries, they assign a status to agriculture equal to that of other sectors of economy. Further, they hold a view that one portion of an economy cannot be happy and prosperous if another is in distress. Karl Brandt holds the view that farmers are a vital part of the arterial system of circulation through which flow the goods and services of the national economy. The nation depends on properly functioning farms as important sources of primary materials, foods and fibres. Yet the farms cannot be treated as an independent object of policies, nor can they be made prosperous in emancipation from the remainder of the economy. He believes that unemployment and decreased output in urban areas cannot be cured by maintaining or restoring economic well-being to the farmers alone. There is still a better explanation of this picture of comparative standing of different sectors which is advanced by T.W. Schultz, W.W. Wilcox and others. According to them, interdependence and close relationship of various sectors of economy or group of economic activities is more important than to say which is more fundamental or which is more important. They say that the size is not the supreme test of importance as the height or weight of a man is no indication of his importance or perstige. The quantitative tests such as the physical volume of output, the amount and the ratio of income to total income and the number of persons engaged in it, etc., are misleading in this regard. In the initial stages of development of any economy, economic, activities may be simple and compartmentalised. When an economy grows further and faster, interdependence of various activities increases and their mutual relationship becomes closer. In its economic evolution when a country grows as an exchange economy, it becomes impossible to establish which sector is more important. It is the mutual stimulus and the reciprocal behaviour of different parts which make the progress possible. The concepts such as self-sufficiency and self-contained economy lose their importance and there will be a greater degree of dependence and cooperation. In this ever changing relationship it is difficult to establish fundamentalism if any.

It is now futile to argue the relative importance of land, labour and capital because progress in modern time is measured by an adequate leisure and an adequate provision of the means enjoying that leisure i.e. consumption goods and services that make life rich and wholesome, in short, worth living. Nevertheless, it is observed in recent years that economic development of India is an inter-disciplinery phenomenon. This seems to be a concluding statement and conveys meaningful connotation if interrelationship of different disciplines or branches when an economy intends to grow. However, India in spite of development efforts for over three decades past, remains still an agriculturally dominant country. It is an established fact that stability of agriculture lends stability to overall economy of India.

Apart from the fact that each sector of an economy is dependent on the other in the modern complex society, it is worth analysing to know how far such sectors are existing or co-existing and to assess to what extent each sector can contribute to the process of economic development. Agriculture, for instance, does play a very significant role in more than one direction. Besides being a source of food which is basic necessity of man, it supplies raw materials for industrial development, its marketable surplus forms a source of capital formation ; a rise in the incomes of the farmers extends the size of market for non-agricultural commodities and products ; one of the sources of labour supply to the industries is agriculture agricultural exports bring foreign-exchange that is necessary for financing development projects ; agricultural class of people forms a major portion of total population of most of the developing countries and as such serves as a backbone of economic, political, social and cultural emancipation of such countries. "Agriculture plays many roles in the processes of economic growth and development, but most of them can be summarized under four headings : (1) providing more food and raw materials, (2) serving as a market for the products of the industrial sector, (3) supplying savings to other sectors of the economy, and (4) providing productive employment."[12]

In the less-developed countries, industrialization commences from utilising agricultural output as input. Number of processing and manufacturing industries are the instances. Rural industries are mainly agro-based industries. Even most of the medium and large-scale industries flourish by producing inputs needed for agricultural development. Thus, industrialization will expand with the help of agricultural raw materials and agriculture in turn will progress with the help of inputs produced by many of the industries. Black-smithy, carpentry, mat-making etc., are the cottage industries ; handlooms, oil extraction, ginning are shall-scale industries ; fertilizers, pesticides, tractors and other machineries are produced by large scale industries. Cotton-textiles, sugar industries, etc. are also the example of big industries.

The role of agriculture in economic development is better illustrated if an analysis of certain theories of Ragnar Nurkse, Arthur Lewis and Ramis-Fei is put forth in this connection. Nurkse while explaining the problems of capital formation in less developed countries brings out how do the wage goods (agricultural products) have a way of balanced growth. It is through the augmentation and distribution of agricultural surplus that breaks the vicious-circle of poverty obtaining in these countries. The concept of balanced growth has been evolved by an analogy of balanced-diet. If agriculture is

12. Economic Development, Clarence Zuvekas, Macmillan International College Edition, 1979, p. 204.

made productive and stable, the growth of an economy is ensured without disturbances or diseqilibria. Nurkse goes on discussing how capital formation in less developed countries takes place by means of surplus wage-goods arising from the agricultural sector and feeding the industries. The process of enlarging the size of market continues, as he says, even by way of foreign trade. Thus all measures that promote agricultural progress have to be undertaken so as to complement industrialization of the countries concerned. Though Nurkse's suggestions involve financial, administrative and practical problems on the part of vulnerable countries such as developing economies, his arguments do have relevance to the significant role to be played by the agricultural sector.

Arthur Lewis, on the other hand, advances his two-sector model stating that capitalist sector expands indefinitely provided agricultural sector remains a subsistence sector. His assumptions of stagnant agriculture, unlimited supply of labour from agricultural sector to the industrial sector, ploughing back all the profits of capitalists in terms of ivestment, etc., do not stand the test of time. Nevertheless, his contentions reflect on the fact that as long as many of the less developed countries are less prone to changes in their agriculture, it is agriculture which promotes the expansion of capitalist sector. In the initial stages of the less-developed countries, of course, the role of agriculture is quite understandable.

Ramis and Fei further probe into the matter of relationship between agriculture and industry and come out with three phases development of the less-developed countries. In the first phase, it is stated that agriculture remains traditional and industry grows at the cost of agriculture by utilising cheap labour coming from the agricultural sector. During the second phase, it is explained that agriculture starts undergoing changes and marginal productivity of labour becomes positive. Surplus labour beigns declining and limiting the indefinite expansion of capitalist sector. In the third phase, both agriculture and industry grow together. Agriculture is counted to be on par with industry. Nevertheless, Ramis and Fei's theory shows how agriculture plays an important role in all the three phases of development. In conclusion, it is apt to quote Schultz "Agriculture may limit severely or contribute importantly to the development of a particular economy".[13] If agriculture is not properly organised and managed, it serves as a bottle-neck for the growth of an economy, whereas if it is made productive and progressive economic development of that country is fostered by agricultural prosperity. 'Improvement in the productivity of agriculture is one of the most solid means of promoting industrialization, in fact unless agriculture does modernise substantially, industrial expansion in most underdeveloped countries is likely to be cut short by lack of markets, for the great majority of the population will not have the necessary purchasing power. Conversely, agricultural improvement cannot go very far unless there is industrial development to take up the released manpower and to provide a solid technical base for the equipment and services essential to modernized agriculture."[14]

In developing countries such as India, accelerating the growth of agricultural output involves a comprehensive package of policies based on clear understanding of inter-relationships, complementaries and conflicts among different policy actions. Technological change is a pre-requisite for the rise in agricultural productivity. The adoption of new technology is intimately tied up with the supply of credit, land tenure structure, the availability of foreign exchange, agricultural research and education, extension services, irrigation, mechanization, transportation, marketing and storage, agricultural sector planning, price policy etc. Of course, this package will vary according to the economic, agronomic and institutional conditions prevailing in each country or region.

Technological change through Green Revolution in India has given us some lessons of experience. In short,

---

13. Economic Organization of Agriculture, by T.W. Schultz.
14. The Future of Underdeveloped Countries, by Eugene Stanley Harper & Brothers, New York, 1954, p. 304.

whatever technology is to be introduced it should fit in the local conditions. Once the technology is adopted and proved to be successful, follow-up measures need to be pursued for sustained growth. New technology does not necessarily mean the technology borrowed from foreign countries.

Technological development precedes agricultural research and education. Sufficient allocation of resources for promoting further research and education is imperative. Consequent upon the technological advancement, extension services and technical guidance have to be ensured to have continuous technical progress.

Any development in the agricultural sector has to be planned properly keeping a wider and longer perspective in view. Agricultural sector planning has to be coordinated and integrated. Well-knit programmes and projects have to form the components of required strategies. As agriculture pursuits in India are not systematically organised and monitored, agricultural planning appears to be a good mechanism and instrument of agricultural development. Agricultural planning has to be implemented in a suitable institutional frame-work mainly depended on tenurial systems. First and foremost requisite of successful planning in agriculture is reformation of land tenures. Of course, land reforms have been already put into practice in a number of states in India. But, degree of their effective implementation differs from State to State. Since tenancy reforms and other agrarian reforms have been in vogue for the last 2 to 3 decades in India, circumstances are changing fast so as to accept these reforms as inevitable institutional arrangements. However, there are certain obstacles which have to be tackled by the government with suitable legislative measures.

Infrastructural changes in the fields of irrigation, transportation, marketing and storage have been figuring with noticeable progress. In order to supply irrigation facilities, numerous irrigation projects—major and minor—have been undertaken and CADAs are effective executive and educative authorities in this connection. Vigorous efforts are in progress to overcome difficulties and obstacles if any in this context.

Urban-rural transport, inter-farm transport, farm to village transport have been improved during the plan-era. Nevertheless, there is much to be done in this direction. Minimum Needs Programme is a novel approach to the development of rural road system. Of course, there is no gain-saying about the importance of transport in rural India. Physical isolation of the villages has to be broken so that the villages are to be brought in the fold of modern communication, information and other urban facilities. This process helps directly and indirectly the growth rate of agricultural production, distribution and consumption.

Marketing of agricultural commodities which is closely connected with transportation has to be improved so as to bring fair and reasonable prices for the farmers. APMCs and other regulated markets are working at present in a slow and relatively to a lesser extent. It is therefore essential that the agricultural marketing has to be well organised by plugging defects of the present system.

Price policy for agricultural stability and growth in very important phenomenon which cannot be easily dispensed with. Agricultural prices are again influenced by the prices of non-agricultural commodities and goods. When the modernised agriculture needs inputs of varied nature many of which originate in industral sector, the prices of such inputs influence the production costs in agricultural sector. Consequently, investment decisions in agricultural sector are shaped by the interactions of prices and costs of products and within itself and outside sector i.e. industrial sector. Again, when the agricultural prices rise due to the rise in agricultural inputs, the product-prices of the industries using agricultural output and produce also increase. As such, the price-policy of agricultural products has to be looked from and linked to the general price-policy. In short, there is an inter-dependence between the agricultural prices and the prices of industrial products and services. Nevertheless, price stability of agricultural produce is very much essential for its progress.

Production credit is a major limiting factor of agricultural development. In the wake of modernising agriculture due to economic development policies, the credit-needs of the farmers grow. In order to meet increasing credit-gap, institutional finance has to be advanced to a satisfactory extent. Though money-lenders still play a predominant role, credit policy has to reduce their importance by releasing required amount of loans through the various banking and financial agencies. Commercial banks, cooperative banks, land development banks and regional rural banks have to be strengthened in their loaning capacities. National Bank for Agricultural and Rural Development has assumed a greater role in this context. Its operations have to be expanded and intensified so as to accelerate the growth process in agricultural sector. Side by side, Integrated Rural Development Programme along with its deviants and associates has to proceed with vigour and efficiency.

In developing economies such as India where population is dense and is growing at a faster rate than in other parts of the world, much of its burden is shared by the agricultural sector. Many-times, agriculture serves as a shock-absorber of unemployment arising from frictional relations in the industrial sector. As such, the development policy of developing economies has to strengthen the agricultural base with efficiency and productivity. In order to do this, two policy measures are necessary. In the first instance, agricultural diversification and intensification of development projects therein open up new and more employment opportunities. Secondly, whichever labour remains in excess by way of disguised unemployment would be absorbed if non-agricultural activities and pursuits increase in the industrial and service sectors. In conclusion, employment generation programmes have to be devised in both agricultural and non-agricultural sectors.

The role of agro-based industries and the industries supplying agricultural inputs such as machines, chemical fertilisers, pesticides etc. is also remarkable. In the developing countries, several industries using agricultural output crop up. With the diversification of the base and foundations of agriculture, the possibility of coming up of such industries is more significant. Similarly, as the agriculture undergoes a change in methods and practices of cultivation, the industries supplying modern inputs and improved requirements of agricultural sector grow in number. Naturally, linkages in between agro-based industries and agro-supply industries are built. These linkages and interdependencies reinforce the growth of agricultural and non-agricultural activities. In short, agricultural sectoral development depends on package of policies inter-linked and interacting in coordinated manner. In the ultimate analysis, it is conditioned by the political will of the Government and favourable response of the peasants.

Apart from the domestic policies for agricultural stability and growth, international commercial policies also help in building the soundness of developing economies. Analysis of the working of international commodity arrangements, international buffer-stock system and food-aid policies has therefore to be looked into so far as this view-point is concerned. Though Indian agriculture at present is considered to be self-sufficient in food-production, sometimes food-shortages arise due to famine and drought conditions as well as unforeseen wars and emergencies. In order to face such situations, international buffer-stock and food-aid arrangements have to be thought of well in advance. It is in this connection, recent UNCTAD deliberations focus attention on building international buffer-stock. Though definite decisions have not been arrived at in respect of many commodities, the proposal of international buffer-stock appears to be a very good solution to the instabilities of backward and underdeveloped agriculture of developing economies. Such buffer-stocks help easing the erratic price-fluctuation and food-shortages that are likely to erupt in the developing economies under such circumstances.

Further, P.L. 480 food-aid of the USA and other food supplying measures of some of the other developed countries including Russia did sway a considerable influence on the Indian agriculture till very recently. Such aid-programmes eased the food-situation of India until the Indian agriculture has proved to be self-sufficient in food-production. Even in respect of other developing countries, food aid and food-grants are believed to breed soothing effects. One caution is always to be kept in mind of the concerned countries that food-aid programmes should not serve as disincentive for the production measures of such countries. Sufficient care also needs to be taken in such a way that food-imports not push up the prices of domestic food-articles and other products. At the same time, food-aid programmes should be treated as ad-hoc arrangements and the domestic agriculture of LDCs should be made self-reliant side-by-side. Similarly, the grants part of the food-aid should be higher so that the LDCs should not suffer the commitment of repayment of interest and loan component of such aid.

Main objectives of the international commodity agreements are : (1) to raise or uphold export-earnings by means of arrangements among producers, restricting production or exports or both; (2) to promote economic stability, both in the producing and in the consuming countries, by preventing under fluctuations of prices and quantities traded but without interfering with long term trends; (3) to mitigate the problems and hardships of such long-term adjustments as may be required in cases of persistent disequilibrium between production and consumption particularly under conditions of inelastic supply and demand; (4) to counteract the shrinkage of markets to primary producers which results from protectionist measures of preferential arrangements in importing countries, and (5) to act as instruments for inter-governmental commodity programming by governments on more comprehensive lines, taking account of trade on both commercial and concessional terms, of national policies relating to production, prices and stocks, and of the close links between problems of commodity trade, aid and development programmes.

The negotiating countries may try to realize one of the five objectives or combination of them. However, one of the chief difficulties in the actual negotiation of international commodity agreements has been that the participating governments have not always been fully conscious of which of these five objectives they were mainly aiming at; nor were they fully conscious of the extent to which any of these objectives could be successfully attained by one or the other of the standard types of agreement techniques. The primary exporting countries have been naturally interested not just in the stability of prices but in securing reasonable returns in terms of the manufactured goods which they are buying-in much the same manner in which the primary producers of the developed countries are mainly interested in obtaining some degree of parity of purchasing power in relation to the rest of the economy. The importing countries, on the other hand, have been mainly interested in securing more stable conditions of trade and have been prepared to consider any measures influencing the levels of exporters' returns, over an average of years, only in so far as such measures formed part of a process of orderly adjustment of production to the changing conditions of the world markets. In particular, it must be recognised that commodity agreements cannot be successful in stabilising prices and in securing reasonable terms of trade unless they also succeed in bringing world productions and consumption into balance. "What is needed is a concerted attack on a number of fronts-long term lending and aid as part a of comprehensive development programme; compensatory finance international agreements for the regulation of production for coordinated planning in the creation of new capacity and for the provision of guarantee of access to markets; long-term purchase agreements, conditional and unconditional, continuing consultations between governments, both commodity by commodity and in close link with wider discussions on trade, aid and development planning including also confrontations of plans of individual countries-all of which should be pursue simultaneously and with vigour."[15]

15. Agriculture in Economic Development, edited by Eicher and Witt, (1st Indian reprint 1970, p. 339.

In conclusion, agriculture has a very significant role to play in accelerating the growth process of developing countries. It produces food for the growing population, it supplies agricultural surplus for financing industrialization; it serves as a source of increasing employment and it earns foreign exchange. Agricultural fundamentalism has no more any meaning than serving as a spring-board for further growth of other sectors such as industry and services. Transforming traditional agriculture into modernised agriculture necessitates institutional and structural changes. It demands the conversion of ignorant and illiterate farmers into enlightened and entrepreneurial class. The domestic policies of agricultural improvement and price-stability have to be closely linked with the growth of world agriculture and international commodity arrangements for price-stability within and outside the developing countries. A concerted and coordinated package of the policies is warranted for avoiding agricultural instabilities of LDCs. The international agencies of development such as FAO, UNO, IMF, UNCTAD etc., are expected to work in a cohesive and complementary manner to erase the defects of underdeveloped agriculture. Ultimately, what is wanted from global point of view is to avoid the imbalances in the growth process of agriculture irrespective of the stage of development of any country in the world. Further, ecological balance and environmental purification should be given proportionate attention in the process of development. Boundary and beauty of the natural resources should be maintained in a commensurate manner to make the world habitable and liveable.

3

Industrialization and Economic Development

At the outset, it appears necessary to thrash out some controversy over industrialization being identified as economic development. It is clear that whenever one talks about economic development, he is likely to count it in terms of the extent of which industrialization has taken place in a particular country. Generally, the distinction between developed and under-developed countries is pointed out by narrating certain examples of industrial super-structure in developed countries and the dearth of such an extent of industrialization in the less developed countries.[16] Further, it is also common to observe that through industrialization national output is rapidly and greatly increased. In the same manner, it is to be mentioned that because of widespread industrial structure, physical infrastructure has been built to promote and facilitate the economic activities of all kinds. Again in order to enlist increasing returns from any economic pursuit, suggesstion is

16. Normally the concepts such as under-developed, less developed and developing economies are used synonymously though there is finer and subtle distinction between these concepts.

always to industrialize that particular occupation. Due to all these and other host of considerations, it is natural to consider economic development as identical with industrialization. However, if one probes in depth of the analysis, it is found out that economic development is a wider connotation than the concept of industrialization.

The other view which explains economic development in its technical and scientific term states that some countries in the world which are not much industrialized but continue to be predominently primary producing countries are rated to be developed countries. For instance, Australia and New Zealand are described to be among the developed nations. Even the most advanced countries like U.S.A. which are affluent and which are in the age of high mass-consumption as per the stage-analysis of W.W. Rostow are facing problem of what is next stage ? These illustrations show that industrialization is not an ultimate objective of economic development. In the case of developing economies where there are many under-utilized resources, industrialization is a prerequisite for further growth and development. On the other hand, regarding highly industrialized countries, future functions of economic development appear to be of far-reaching and long-lasting in addition to industrialization. If there is a declining rate of profit in respect of mature industries, what is needed is further invention, a function of human ingenuity. A state of affairs such as recession calls for extended functions of bureaucrats, technocrats policymakers. industrialists, entrepreneurs and above all research personnel of top-cadre to get it remedied. In case of some industries facing lock-outs, strikes etc. managerial and extension personnel are to be tuned up to ensure harmonious industrial relations for promoting industrial peace. All these and other number of considerations show that there is a tremendous role to be played by service-sector (human capital) including agents and agencies mentioned above. Thus, the connotation and process of economic development are wider and greater than what seems to be by way of industrialization. Nevertheless, the role of industrialization is very significant both in developed and developing economies from a number of points of view. Let us examine them in proceeding paragraphs.

Initial step to distinguish agriculture from industry starts usually with comparing 'Farm' with 'Firm'. Of course, industry is nothing but group of firms of similar nature. 'Farm' is usually a unit of operation for a particular industry as 'firm' is a unit of operation for agriculture. Though both farm and firm have similar objective of making their operations profitable, the farm does have severe limitations such as limited supply of land, vagaries of weather conditions, dearth of entrepreneurial capacity and other risks and uncertainties. Primarily, farm operations are undertaken to cater to the needs of farm families and afterwards such operations are extended to meet the market requirements ; whereas the firm carries its operations primarily to meet the demands of the markets. Its operations are further conducted to cater to the needs of international markets. Of course, of late the farms started producing for the international markets. Even then as it will be seen later, their share in international market is less than that of industrial products. Besides, as it is already seen in the foregoing chapter that agricultural prospects in international markets are not so optimistic. However, the role of agriculture in economic development needs not be considered as less significant as is evident in the preceding chapter.

For all practical and analytical purposes, industry is taken to mean manufacturing industry. "The underdeveloped regions have long been mainly producers of raw materials, and they have observed that there is a strong and positive connection between the wealth and standard of living of a country and the extent of its industrialization. They also see that as prices for raw materials fluctuate much more than prices of manufactured goods, an economy which is dependent on the export of one or a few basic commodities suffers from instability of the national income more than economies which are industrialized and more self-sufficient. Observing these faults, the people of the under-developed countries have naturally come to believe that, in order to achieve greater security, stability and a higher standard of living, their countries must become industrialized".[17] The notion

17. Industrial Development by Murray D. Bryce (International Student Edition), 1960, McGraw Hill Book Company, Inc, pp. 3-4.

of industrialization as understood by the underdeveloped countries is characterised by such industries as are capital intensive and having large size plants. Instead of entering the controversy over different types of industries that are suitable to the less developed countries, it is better to put forth the arguments in general taking industrialization in toto. The fact that why industrialisation is preferred, is answered by stating that it accommodates investment of any size in a number of technological developments. These investments do breed increasing returns through the instruments of external and internal economies. Since human needs are unlimitedly increasing, it is through industrialization emanated from inventions and innovations, such needs are being met. As it is, natural resources abounding in any economy have to be exploited in a scientific manner and industrialization is accepted to be a process of such utilization of the natural resources. What human hands cannot do will be done by the machines. As such it is possible to turn out on large-scale such products as are required in large quantities and numbers. The relationship of industrialization to economic development has been described by Gunnar Myrdal as following :

"Manufacturing industry represents in a sense, a higher stage of production. In advanced countries the development of manufacturing industry has been concomitant with these countries, spectacular economic progress and rise in levels of living ; many of its products are indeed almost symbolic of a high living standard. Not least in the underdeveloped countries, the productivity of manpower in industry tends to be considerably greater than in the traditional agricultural pursuits. Industrialization and the growth of that part of the working population that is engaged in industry is therefore a means of raising national income per capita. In countries like India and Japan, with a high ratio of population to natural resources and, in particular, to land, manufacturing industry represents vitrtually the only hope of greatly increasing labour productivity and raising levels of living, however much is done to improve agriculture. But even in countries where the population pressure is lower—as for example in many Latin American countries—the successful exploitation of a more favourable relation between population and natural resources requires mostly the growth of manufacturing industry"[18]. As is already mentioned, industry augments national income. If an industrial project fails to make a positive contribution to the national income, it is almost certain to be a cause of reducing the national income. Such an industrial project may be worthwhile for non-economic reasons ; then it has to find its justification apart from the general principle which should guide the industrial progress as a whole.[19] Apart from increasing the national income, industrialization earns foreign exchange by way of exports. It provides for employment. It also serves as a market for agricultural products and exploits usable and unused resources whether human or material to their full economic potential.

To enlist advantages of industrialization, it is necessary to know what should be the characteristic of sound industrial projects and in what pattern such industries should come about. One of the pre-requisites of having projects run on sound lines is to have assured and already existing market either at home or abroad. This condition minimizes the risks of finding out necessary market after a particular industry is established. Secondly, proposed industries should have a prospective advantage in production costs compared to foreign or domestic competitors. Finally, the industries that are going to be started should be such as to meet the felt-needs of a growing economy and fit in the long-term economic trends of the country concerned. If a project is to have long-term value to developing economy, it will have certain characteristics which grow out of the complex relationships in the economy. These characteristics are excellently described in the manual "How to select Dynamic Industrial

---

18. An Internationl Economy, by Gunnar Myrdal, Harper and Brothers, New York, 1956, p. 226.

19. Industrial Development by M.D. Bryce, 1960. (International Student Edition), p. 266.

Projects" published by the International Cooperation Administration of U.S.A.[20]

"An industrial project...must mesh into the economy as the latter is now constituted and operating in the sense that it must draw its necessary inputs from the existing or immediately potential sectors of the economy and imports, and it must see immediate, expanding markets to support industry or to supply ultimate consumers. Second, besides functioning as part of the present structure of the economy, it must fit underneath the next phase of economic development, either supplying consumers with goods they need in that phase, supplying investment goods for the investment activity in that phase, supplying an input or inputs into other productive activities in that phase, or providing an export with which to pay for imports in that phase. This linkage of the project with both the present and the future, looking back to its inputs and forward to expanded future markets, is a feature possessed only by the truly dynamic and profitable industrial projects at any particular time". Sound industrial projects for a developing region not only need to be technically and economically sound, they should also be able to produce early profits for both the investor and the economy. They should also fit in with the long-term trends and needs of the growing economy.

It is difficult to find out sound industrial projects especially in the developing economies. However, such promising industrial development projects often have to be discovered by development agencies and then offered to businessmen who may undertake them. How to identify them depends on a number of industrial opportunities that can be traced by different approaches. Though there is a need of intensive and thorough investigation to determine economic, technical and financial soundness of such projects as well as their value to the economy, some broad guidelines for ascertaining the prospective and promising industrial projects include a

20. Quoted by M.D. Bryce in his book "Industrial Development", p. 16.

nvestigation of local markets, (b) study of imports for assessing the proven demand, (c) using of available skills for new openings, (d) thorough study of existing industries for sake of diversification, (e) applying new technologies, (f) examining the inter-industry relationship and dependence, (g) evaluation of development plan; so as to find out surrounding opportunities, (h) review of old projects to find out new opportunities in the old ideas, (i) observing experience of similar industrial developments in the other countries or regions having somewhat similar conditions, and (j) use of industrial classification done by U.N.O. or Planning Commission of India or other international standard classification already accepted or recommended as check-list of opportunities. In spite of these various key-points for adopting or installing industrial projects, certain non-economic considerations are followed in developing economies due to political pressures or prestige point of view or age-old traditional values towards different occupations. Such situations cause a number of errors committed in the view of industrialization of these countries. It is therefore pertinent to caution the investors both private and public by quoting Maurice Zinken.[21] The question that planners ask in Asia is not "how can the national income...be increased the most at least cost?" Instead they begin from a whole series of different premises and build upon them. They argue that wealth comes from industrialization; so they create uneconomic industries and bolster them with protection. They accept that national safety requires a high degree of autarchy; so they build up defence industries which run expensively because their production is too small. They consider that the handicraftsman represents certain social values which are important to preserve; so they keep him in existence by subsidies. They worry about their balance of payments; so they lend money to shipping companies at uneconomically low rates, or talk of synthetic petrol plants. They have the political pressures on their Ministers to consider; so they spread schemes evenly over the country and give special attention to backward

21. Development for Free Asia, Chatto and Windus, London, 1956, p. 44, quoted by M.D. Bryce in his book "Industrial Development".

areas...The list of errors into which the ignoring of profit leads is long. Separately they can each be justified by some non-economic consideration, from defence to human charity. Together they are keeping the people of Asia in poverty and squalor and ignorance for longer than necessary.

In the same fashion, certain white-elephant plants are economically unsound projects. They are not only too much strenuous on the part of public exchequer, but also such plants are not wanted from the point of productivity and value to their national economies. However, the developing economies install them to show to other countries that such plants are prestigeous. Instead of spending hundreds of crores of rupees on such plants, these countries could have as well financed many projects that are needed by their economies imminently as well as perspectively.

Pattern of Industrialization

The pattern of industrialization is to be viewed from the point of view of ownership, size and nature of technologies. General controversy about ownership is between state vs private enterprise. Again the different technologies such as capital intensive, labour-intensive, intermediate technologies, etc., influence the nature and mode of industrialization. The notion of size of plants forms the other kind of analysis. In particular, problems and prospects of different size of plants pose peculiar challenges for the less-developed countries.

Until 1930s depression, private investors and entrepreneurs played a very commendable role in shaping the industrialization of developed countries. It is through this type of capitalism industrial-super-structure became a usual feature of such countries. However, after the failure of capitalism i.e. private enterprise during the period of depression, many governments started thinking of state-ownership and entrepreneurship. Especially in the less-developed countries, the state-ownership has been expanding rapidly. It is quite understandable when peculiar situation obtaining in such countries is looked into. In these developing economies, private enterprise has not been soundly organised and developed. Its resources are also limited in view of huge size of investment needed for financing a larger number of development projects. Besides, risks and uncertainties of such projects are not conducive to the fostering of private entrepreneurship. Regarding decision-taking process, it is believed that public enterprises are more efficient than the private enterprises. In respect of public enterprises, policy decision is usually taken as per the advice of expert body such as Planning Commission. It is the pool of calibres that influences the decision making which is almost more correct and efficient than the decision taken by individuals as in the case of private enterprises. Private enterprises are motivated by the objective of profit maximization whereas the public enterprises are based on the motive of social welfare maximization. The developing economies which were colonies earlier are more concerned with the welfare-maximization principle. Hence, there happens to be the increasing role for state ownership of industries in less developed countries. It is quite a long time for many of the old industries such as cotton-textiles in India which need to be rationalised. For rationalization of such industries, there is a need of huge investment which the private entrepreneurs in these countries cannot afford. As the less-developed countries are backward areas in the sense of physical infrastructure, the development of social over-head capital including public utility industries require very large size of investment which again cannot be provided for by the private investors. From the foregoing considerations it is clear that in less developed countries public sector industries are likely to expand to a greater extent than the private sector industries. However, it is gratifying to note that many of the developing economies are mixed-economies where both public sector and private sector are supposed to coexist. Nevertheless, proper measures are to be undertaken to strike compromise between these two sectors so that both sectors would contribute to the development of an economy. Of course, Indian industrial policy allows for the continuance of both sectors for facilitating the development of the country as a whole.

Where the national output has to be increased at a faster speed, large-size industries are established. But at the same time, small-scale and rural industries do have a significant place in the case of developing economies to cater to the needs of rural economy. Especially in India, the policy of industrial development has been striving to promote such industries by way of giving a number of incentives for them. However, there is still a need to coordinate the interests of all types of industries in an integrated manner. Industries are again classified according to the nature of technologies. In less-developed countries where labour is abundant, labour-intensive industries are generally advocated. However, to pick up the required rate of growth of national income capital intensive industries are also established. In the countries such as India where rural sector is larger, small scale and rural industries which use indigenous technology need to be geared to the trends of development. As such, there is an advocacy for intermediate technology in such industries suiting to the technical standards and financial resources of rural entrepreneurs. It is worth noting that India has provided for a number of concessions and incentives for the spread of industries in rural areas.

Recent trends of industrial development both in developing and developed countries point towards the controversy over foreign private investment and foreign public investment. Since most of the developing economies need increasing finance for keeping up the wide-spread industrialization in their economies, the need for foreign private investment arises. Though private investment in these countries is thin in recent years due to fear of nationalization and other restrictions imposed on the flow of such funds, multi-national corporations do sway an impressive influence on the part of these less-developed countries. The Multi-National Corporations do supplement the industrial development in the developing countries by way of assigning more capital, modern technology and expert personnel. However, there MNCs are taken with hesitation by these countries thinking that such corporations tend to strengthen the economic and technical efficiency of the developed countries' large investors and weaken the sovercignty of the developing economies and upset the perspective expectations of industrialization of their economies. Next issue of capital flows in the developing economies for promoting their industrialization, relates to foreign-aid and lending policies of the international development financing agencies. Of course, the countries such as India are trying to reduce their reliance on foreign-aid. Nevertheless, these countries ask for increasing assistance from the international agencies at concessional or reduced rate of interest and a larger number of instalments of repayment spread over a longer period of time.

Taking into account certain problems arising in international field regarding the future course of industrialization in developed and developing economies, it is found out that the developed countries started protecting their industries from the adverse effects of inflation, unemployment, recession and competition from other countries. On the other hand, the developing economies began establishing import substitution industries and asking for the entry of their manufactured goods in the markets of the developed countries. These ceuntries appeal to the developed countries for encouraging them to form the regional integration of the less developed countries. Besides, the international organisations such as IBRD, IDA, IMF, GATT & UNCTAD are persuaded to devise some suitable policies which can promote industrialization in these countries. Nevertheless, there are genuine problems of industrialization faced by the developing economies. For instance, demarcation of economic activities between large-scale and, small-scale and village industries is a major problem yet to be settled. The problem of extent to which labour-intensive industries are to be spread bothers these countries. Financing of very many industries with limited domestic resources poses another important problem. Since trade-unions in less developed countries are not organised on sound and healthy lines, management and labour relations problem also proves to be an obvert problem. Because of increasing social costs of industrial location in big cities, problem of decentralization is to be considered the most concerned problem. The problem of pricing in public enterprises and private enterprises has to be viewed from the points of social welfare criteria as against economic efficiency criterion. Over and above, the problem of coordination of the public enterprises and private enterprises in a number of fields remains to be solved. As already mentioned, the problems of joint-ventures, multinational corporations and white-elephant projects do merit serious consideration of these less-developed countries

In conclusion, the prima facie case for industrialization is readily set out:[22] "First, developed countries have industry; therefore the way to become developed is to industrialize. (This is a fallacy of the *post hoc ergo propter hoc* variety, but it carries a powerful appeal to under-developed countries). Second, the marginal value product of labour is higher in industry than in agriculture; to transfer a worker from agriculture to industry raises national output. This is especially the case when disguised unemployment exists in agriculture, so that any product out of a transferred worker in industry is better than none on the farm. Third, industrialization has external ecnomies, whereas agriculture has not. These reside in training, in stimulating communication, interaction, demonstration effects in production as well as consumption, and so on. Rural society tends to be stagnant; urban society dynamic. Industrialization brings urbanization, therefore it is better than the stimulation of agriculture. Fourth, the improvement of agriculture waits on the availability of manufactured inputs such as fertilizer and farm machinery. In order to increase efficiency on the farm one must start in the factory".

Though countries do not develop by industry alone, industrialization is a key to faster development. A successful strategy for industrial progress has to deal with a variety of problems. In most of the developing countries, there are a host of problems, namely, (1) lack of sound financial markets,

22. Economic Development (International Student 2nd edition, by C.P. Kindlerberger), p. 213.

(2) shortage of credit, (3) shortage of skilled and middle level manpower, (4) lack of sufficient entrepreneurial skills, (5) electric power shortage, (6) lack of proper incentives for export of manufactures, and for expansion of manufacturing sector, (7) inadequate technical assistance to small scale and cottage industries, (8) absence of effective measures for redistribution of income, and (9) low urge for regional economic integration.

For mobilising adequate savings for promoting economic development, there is a need for sound financial and money markets. In most of the developing countries, security markets are rudimentary and some times non-existent. Life insurance institutions do not attract large number of people. Mortgage lending and loan associations are few and far between. It is therefore necessary that the Government should devise suitable policies to strengthen the financial markets. Development Finance Corporations and other financial intermediaries should be encouraged and necessary incentives may also be built to form such of them in private sector also.

Another related problem is shortage of industrial credit for plant construction and purchase of machinery and equipment. This problem has to be met by establishing development banks. As a short-run measure, private foreign investment as well as foreign public lending may be sought after.

Skilled labourers and middle level workers are short of supply in most of the developing countries. Government can overcome this shortage by changing their educational policies to conform more closely with development objectives. They can also subsidize on-the-job training which is frequently less costly than technical education in secondary and post-secondary institutions.

The role of entrepreneurial class has been much emphasized by Hirshman, Schumpeter and Leibenstein. It is this class which bears risks of initiating any new innovation that is strategically required for economic development. Import of such persons from abroad becomes political and does appear to be a long-term solution. Therefore, the government may create incentives for private industries by way of advancing supervised credit and through special training programmes for owner-operators of small and medium size industrial firms. Side by side, the government itself should assume entrepreneurial role for priority industries and wherever private sector is shy.

Electric power shortage many times hampers industrial firms to operate up to their maximum capacity. Of course, there are hydro-electric power plants in India, but they are not in adequate number to meet the power requirements. Besides, rural electrification also consumes lot of the power generated. However, the role of power in pushing up the rate of industrial growth cannot be dismissed too lightly. As such more and more allocation of resources for power-generation is necessary for faster rate of growth of an economy.

Lack of incentives for export of manufactures is another limiting factor. Since manufacturers in developing countries often have little access to good information on overseas markets and markets are imperfect in other ways, special incentives are necessary and desirable to stimulate exports of manufactured goods. It is gratifying to note that at present India is in a position to export some of the industrial products. At this juncture, special attention has to be given to encourage the exports of manufactured goods and products. In addition to stimulating cost-cutting measures, following are some of the incentive measures in that direction:[23]

1. Special export credit facilities to provide working capital to exporters, to give them cash between the date of shipment and their receipt of payment, and to enable them to extend credit to their customers.

---

23. Economic Development, Clarence Zuvekas, 1979, p. 257.

2. Export credit insurance to cover both commercial and political risks.

3. Identification of market opportunities which individual firms have difficulty of discovering on their own.

4. Participation in international trade fairs to publicize the country's products, to scout the competition; and to learn what potential buyers are demanding in terms of product standardization, delivery schedules, and other non-price aspects of the demand size of the market.

5. Training for commercial attaches assigned to embassies in major importing countries.

6. Provision of export subsidies and other financial incentives.

7. Correction of over valued exchange rates to make exports more attractive to importing countries.

8. Reduction of bureaucratic red tape in the application for export licenses and processing of export documentation. The process is sometimes so long and costly that it constitutes a major barrier for potential exporters.

A great deal of assistance is now available, however, from the United Nations Industrial Development Organisation, other U.N. agencies and foreign aid agencies. The developing countries can avail of such technical expertise and financial assistance.

Particularly in India where there are a large number of small scale and cottage industries, industrialization cannot speed smoothly unless such industries are made viable. In order to make them complementary to the large-scale industries, suitable technical assistance and other incentives are necessary. As these industries generate more employment opportunities, they play a very important role in India where additional labour force is increasing considerably. Even the technical standard of such industries is low and befitting the local conditions, small scale industries, rural artisans and other cottage industries should be encouraged. Further, certain improvements upon the existing method of production are called for. Other measures of adopting and popularising intermediate technology are to be devised and promoted to a greater extent. Export promotion measures of making the products of such industries attract more and more foreign markets have to be found out.

What is more distressing in this context is lack of increasing purchasing power of the people to consume the products of large-scale and small scale industries. When national income distribution measures are undertaken in such a way that increasing number of poor and weaker sections get more and more income, sufficient marketing potentialities are ensured.

In recent times, it is observed that regional trade blocks are formed to benefit their member countries. This sort of development in international trade has become imperative on the part of the developing countries when they are facing competition from the developed countries. Though there are many advantages of the regional integration or cooperation, the experience uptil now indicates that the political will necessary to make such cooperation successful is generally lacking in the developing countries. "It is useful to emphasize again that industrialization programme in developing countries can easily run into foreign exchange bottlenecks. Unless close attention is paid to this constraint and to the potential of the agricultural sector for overcoming it through food import substitution and exports industrial growth will be forced to slow down."[24]

---

24. Economic Development, Clarence Zuvekas, 1979, p. 264.

4

Service Sector In Economic Development

(Human Resources for Economic Development)

Economic development is a resultant of harmonious utilization of natural resources, financial resources and human resources. The study of interaction between agricultural growth and non-agricultural growth in the process of economic development does therefore lead to the discussion about the role of human resources in economic development. Man is an agent of establishing the interaction and in trun he is bound to interact in between agricultural and non-agricultural activities. It is in this connection necessary to assess to what extent the man is expected to transform or to transcend himself so as to be conducive to the development process. In the earlier chapter it is observed that farm management and industrial management both being the functions of human factor, are considered to be very crucial strategies for promoting economic development especially of the less-developed countries. In consequence, it is imperative to dwelve into the detailed analysis of (a) what is the present nature and size of human resources ? (b) what is needed to transform human resources (i.e. critical choices of investment) into human capital ? (c) what sort of man-power is required (manpower planning) in shouldering the tasks of economic development ? and (d) how far is the manpower planning an integral part of the national planning in India ? and so on.

The developing economies such as of India are rich in human resources in a sense these countries are thickly populated and there is a larger proportion of younger generation. Many times these countries are described as young countries because the bottom of population prism is broader than that obtaining in advanced countries. Besides, the young generation of population has definitely a potentiality of contributing to the economic development for a longer period than the aging population of developed nations. However, at present this young population is looked down as pressure on the available resources of developing economies. This is so because sufficient investment has not been channelized to convert this population into such a class of people who would be capital assets in due course of time. Even the people in the productive age-group are not properly geared to the tasks of development. The aged ones are also not made economically self-dependent by devising old-age welfare measures such as old-age pension programme, health-care measures and other measures so as to reduce their dependency on the earning members of their families. Due to these and other hosts of reasons, there is a tremendous wastage of human resources in the less-developed countries.

Though investment in young generation assumes a huge size and involves a longer gestation period, it brings increased returns in future in such a manner as to compensate more than the austerity suffered by the present generation. Again, the people of productive age group are likely to be more efficient and productive provided sufficient incentives are given to them by way of good teaching, technical education, better extension methods, effective demonstration, in service or on-the-job training, inculcation in them of modern research findings, and encouraging scales and grades of payment of remuneration, etc. The dependency of the aged will be reduced by restructuring the social values, proper design of accumulating necessary savings from their service to finance them at their aging period, devising appropriate measures of putting the aged on such services that would be of some use for some time at least in promoting the economic development, etc. As an evidence, the investment in human resources in U.S.A. during a specific period of time has been found to be a source of contributing to the rise in national income and productivity of the economy[25], (Schultz, T.W.) Further, it is observed that the investment in human resources development accelerates the overall growth process. Accordingly, the investment made in this context enhances the research and inventive qualities of the people which are critically missing at present in the case of less-developed countries. Secondly, competence of the people to shoulder the challenges of development grows through investment in formal and informal educational system. The formal education is imparted in the schools, colleges, Universities and other institutions created for this purpose. The informal education is given by means of social education, adult education, discourses, discussions, demonstrations, crash-programmes of generating employment, etc. Finally, the investment in health programmes as part of human resources development increases the longevity of life, productivity of the employees, hygiene of the people, and reduces the occurrence of diseases, disabilities and the mortality rate in general.

How to derive the benefits from investment in human resources depends on what critical choices of investment are to be made in this context in the process of economic development ? These critical choices are in turn influenced by the objectives of national planning. For instance, in the field of education there are a number of alternatives, namely, (a) investment in producing arts-graduates vs investment in producing science graduates, (b) investment in teacher-training programmes vs others, (c) investment in mass-education vs that in selective group education, (d) investment in institutional

25. Schultz, T.W. "Capital Formation By Education", Journal of Political Economy, Vol. 67, No. 6, pp. 571-583, December 1960.

education vs that in informal education, (e) investment in research vs that in general type of informative education, (f) investment in government-run education vs that in privately-run education, (g) investment in religious or moral education vs that in modern type of education, (h) investment in promoting knowledge vs that in health-programmes and others.

In the fields of health and housing again, there are so many choices to be made so as to fit in the needs of a particular country. Of course, the health programmes in general have to be revamped as per the objectives of development. But in respect of health-programmes also, a series of alternative choices is noticed. For instance, (a) investment in curable diseases vs that in incurable ones, (b) investment in adult health programmes vs that in child health ; (c) investment in applied nutrition programmes vs others, (d) investment in expected mothers vs that in reduction of infant mortality and others. In the sphere of housing, there are several, choices in between : (a) vertical erection of building and horizontal type, (b) cement-concrete and other types of building, (c) supply of houses by government and that by other agencies, (d) housing for the rich and housing for the poor, (e) housing for the organised sector employees and that for employed in unorganised sector and others.

Though human resources development involves investment in education, health and housing, general approach towards this problem has been by way of improving educational system of a country. Because, it is through education that the people learn to live healthily and in a comfortable manner. The investment in health and housing are generally taken care of in the process of human capital formation. Thus, presently our analysis is confined to see the various dimensions of human capital formation and manpower planning. Educational system differs from one stage of development to another stage of development of a particular country. Broadly, objectives of education differ from one country to another when it is looked from the point of stages of growth. According to Meier and Harbison, education in the advanced countries is reasearch and invention oriented whereas in the less developed countries it is towards consolidation of sovereignty and nationalism. In between these two types of countries there are other countries which have different objectives of educational development ranging from the promotion of technical education by strengthening physical science-faculties up to encouraging liberal type of education that creates persons for general administration. Though these are distinguishing features of the educational systems prevailing in different countries all over the world, it is generally accepted that the good and sound educational system needs to incorporate all these features irrespective of the level and stage of development at which a particular country is placed. Only question remains how this good and sound education has to be put into vogue at a rapid rate without further loss of time on the part of developing countries in particular ?

As already mentioned, every nation has to make critical devices suiting its objectives of development. If all the choices are to be accommodated since each choice has its own contribution to economic development, each country has to decide the proportion in which investible funds are to be allotted to each of these choices. The allocation of resources likewise depends on the urgency of each choice. For instance if a country is just freed from colonialism, preference of supplying administrators to technical personnel weighs heavily in respect of that country. On the other hand, if a country is fully advanced in the sense that proper manpower planning has been practised, emphasis of investment in education lies on promotion of research and invention. While a particular country carries its administration and other development projects with the help of short-term training programmes priority of investment naturally runs in favour of long-lasting institutional infrastructure of the educational base. In the same fashion it is to stress that wherever the institutions producing arts-graduates are in more number, policy shift will be in establishing the institutions producing science-graduates. If a particular country does have a high level of intellectuals but at the same time there is shortage of good and sound health of theirs, investment preference goes usually to the health-promoting type of education. Supposing a country is rated as a highly developed country in every aspect except that of moral values, the educational system has to promote moral education as a part of the total curriculum of the academic institutions. In view of huge dimensions of the desired nature of education, if a country falls short of adequate funds, such a country has to promote privately-run educational institutions of course with the same objectives as the nation proclaims side by side the state-owned institutions meant for educational development. However, an urgency of a critical choice has to be matched by appropriate strategy of investment in educational purposes.

After deciding the critical areas of choice of investment in human resources, problem of manpower planning has to be looked into keeping in view the manpower requirements of a particular country. As it is, normal or usual principle believes that the manpower planning is to gear the supply of manpower to its demand. The manpower planning therefore involves the assessment of manpower availability at present and in future. That what type of manpower is required in future depends on two considerations. One aspect of assessment of future requirement is to pinpoint the deficiencies or shortages that are observed in the present man-power supply. Second consideration points towards the size and proportion of the manpower required in future depending on the new tasks and challenges of the developement of a particular economy. In order to ascertain the nature and quantum of presently available man-power in different vocations, necessary efforts have to be made by way of survey, census, culling out of information from both documentary sources and other informal sources. For future supply of man-power an attempt has to be made to quantify the required type of personnel in existing as well as up coming projects and programmes that undergo expansion and need more and more qualified people. The projects that are potential reflect their probable needs of certain type of human resources. For instance, in case of India if environmental purification programme is to be launched in future, the said problem has many dimensions and requires different types of personnel. It is therefore necessary to project such personnel and to devise measures for supplying such people.

In order to produce required manpower, proper investment planning is to be carved out within the given framework of national planning. It means, in other words, manpower planning needs to be integrated into the national planning. It has to be made a part and parcel of the overall planning of the concerned country.

The strategy of integrating manpower planning into the aggregate planning of a nation is understandable when the relationship between population growth and economic development is studied. Higher the proportion of duly educated people in the total population of any country, greater is the rate of development of that country. The rate at which raw content (i.e. illiteracy) of population is disappearing does point out the rate at which a particular country develops. Hence, main objective of development of any developing economy should be to achieve a rapid rate of human capital formation.

Let us see what is human capital formation? How it is measured ? and etc. Though there has been an absence of theoretical model to include human capital in explaining economic development, recent studies and some eminent economists of this century have shown that human capital along with physical capital and others is also one of the determinants of economic development especially of the less developed countries. Importance of human capital was recognised by the classical and neo-classical economists. But, they were unequivocal in their treatment of knowledge, skill and dexterity embodied in human beings as capital goods. They did not include human capital in their theoretical framework. Nevertheless, during this twentieth-century it is Irvin Fisher who laid the analytical foundation of human capital in his book, "The Nature of Capital and Income" as early as 1906. However, the effective treatment of the concept of human capital has been initiated after 1950s by Schultz,[26] and Kuznet[27].

Adam Smith conceived of fixed capital consisting among other things, "of the acquired and useful abilities of all the inhabitants or members of the society",[28] He stretched his idea of labour in treating the human capital formation as its resultant. Alfred Marshall also placed more emphasis on the concept of human investments. He visualized investment in human beings as a total investment in eduation and family care. He went a step ahead and observed "The most valuable of all capital is that invested in human beings;......"[29] It was J.R. Walsh who attempted to measure investment in human beings through formal education. He conceived of education as an investment cultivated for gain.[30] According to Schultz, acquired abilities of man that augment his economic productivity are then elevated to the role of a capital good. Conceding that human investments are difficult to measure exactly, he includes five major categories of activities that improve on human capabilities, viz. health facilities and services, training-the job, formal education adult education and migration of individuals and families.[31] Simon Kuznets also observed that exclusion of human capital in the definition of capital is partial aud narrow. "......the concept of capital and capital formation should be broadened to include investment in health, education and training of the population itself, that is investment in human beings".[32] The contribution of human capital to economic growth and change is now considered to be substantial, both

26. Theodore W. Schultz, "Investment In Human Capital," American Economic Review, Vol. LI, No.1, March 1961.

27. Simon Kuznets, 'Capital In The American Economy and Its Formation and Financing' NBER, Princeton University Press, 1961.

28. Adam Smith 'The Wealth of Nations' Report 1957, p. 247.

29. Alfred Marshall 'Principles of Economics', 1961, p. 564.

30. J.R. Walsh "Capital Concept Applied to Man" Quarterly Journal of Economics, February 1935, p. 257.

31. Schultz: op. cit.

32. Simon Kuznets, op. cit.

as an independent residual factor and as a complement to other inputs. In particular the following aspects of human resources development which is in other words described as human capital formation (HCF) may be gleaned from the earlier writings.[33]

i) In spite of the assumptions of the homogeneity of labour, knowledge and skill are taken to influence productivity.

ii) Education is taken to be fixed capital similar to physical capital.

iii) Education is cultivated for economic gain and a return on it is expected.

iv) In addition to the ordinary return, a risk premium may be paid because of the uncertainty involved in human investments.

v) Nutrition and health care also lead to human capital formation and influence productivity as evidenced by subsistence wage theories.

vi) Family care in the rearing of children are parental investments in future productivity.

vii) Efficiency of adult labour depends not only on embodied capital of the labourer, but also on the supportive capital embodied in the rest of the family members, especially the spouse.

viii) Education is a joint product and has both consumption and investment aspects.

In brief, human resource development (HCF) includes such forces and factors as augment human capabilities and competence. They are grouped into five main categories i.e. research and development, education proper, training, health and migration. Human resource development is the process

---

33. Alexander V. Alex 'Human Capital Approach to Economic Development', Metropolitan 1983, p. 11.

of increasing the knowledge, the skills and the capabilities of all the people in a society. In economic terms, it could be described as the accumulation of human capital and its effective investment in the development of an economy. In political terms, human resource development prepares people for adult participation in political processes, particularly as citizens in a democracy. From the social and cultural points of view, the development of human resources helps people to lead fuller and richer life less bound by tradition. In short, the processes of human resource development unlock the door of modernization.[34]

After understanding the meaning, nature and norm of human resources development (HCF), it is worthwhile to know certain approaches towards measuring contribution of H.C.F. to economic development. In this connection, recent efforts are made to incorporate investments in education into the mainstream of economic analysis. In other words, investment in man is identified with investment in education. The concept of education is also broadened by having included in the educational system such necessary components as research and development, education proper (formal), training, health and technological development that facilitates occupational and spatial mobility of manpower (labour force). All these components have been taken by Schultz, Kuznets Marshall and others to constitute what is called as human resources development or human capital formation. In view of these considerations, broader perspective of education serves as an accepted measure of economic development. The principal approaches that have been adopted in measuring contribution of human capital to economic development are as following: (1) determination of the relationship between expenditure on education and growth in income or in physical capital formation over a period of time in a country: (2) the residual approach in determining

34. Frederick Harbison and Charles A. Myres 'Education Manpower and Economic Growth' Oxford & IBH Publishing Co., Second Indian Reprint, *1970*, p. 2.

the contribution of education to gross national produce (GNP), (3) calculation of the rate of return from expenditure on education; and (4) making inter-country correlations of school enrollment ratios and GNP.

(1) So far as the relationship between expenditure on education and in physical capital formation, Schultz estimated that investment in education in U.S.A. (1950-1956) contributed 3.5 times more than investment in physical capital.

(2) Under assumptions of a linear homogeneous production function and a neutral technical change which does not affect the rate of substitution between capital and labour, Robert M. Solow thus computed a "residual" equal to 87.5 per cent of the increase in output per man hour in the United States between 1909 and 1949.

(3) According to Gary S. Becker rates of return for urban white males in the U.S.A. were 12.5 per cent in 1940 and 10 per cent in 1950. E.F. Renshaw[35] calculated an average return to education, in the U.S.A., of between 5 and 10 per cent over the period 1900 and 1950.

(4) Svennilson, Edding and Elvin came to the following conclusion "...it is obvious that a country with a low GNP per capita cannot afford to have most of its young people between 16 and 19 in full time education and thus withheld from gainful employment. On the other hand, a highly industrialized country with a high GNP per capita can hardly afford to break off the education of most of its young people at the age of 14. Moreover, in a rich country there is high demand for education as current consumption and the margin of income available to satisfy this demand is large."[36]

---

35. E.F. Renshaw "Estimating the Return to Education," Review of Economics and Statistics, August 1960, pp. 318-324.

36. Ingvar Svennilson, Frederich Edding and Lionel Elovin 'Targets for Education in Europe in 1970, vol II-Policy Conference on Economic Growth and Investment in Education, OECD, Paris, January 1962.

In spite of various attempts that have been made to measure the contribution of education to economic development, there are many difficulties of calculation in precise and accurate manner. "The Economic Analysis of investment in man which have been made recently, though representing a significant contribution to economic theory, are of little use as yet to planners, except perhaps to highlight the general importance of education and to suggest that some of the outlyas for education could be considered as investment rather than simply current consumption or social expenditures".[37]

Human Resource Development Policy

It is already proved that human resource development is a joint-product. It therefore needs a unified and coordinated approach. "Investment in human capital takes place in a person and the embodied nature of this capital makes it imperative to treat the human resource development programmes as a single unit. The policy decisions for human resource development program pertain to the allocation of resources for investments in human beings in the form of education, training and health. The demand for these programs vary depending on such factors as age, sex, region and income. Despite these variations in investments, human resource development demands a single policy approach to it."[38] Consequently, educational planning has to be devised in a wider perspective. "Educational planning should largely consist of action designed to move the real world closer to the right end of the continuum, characterized by a multi-policy of alternatives in producing and utilizing educated manpower. For whatever is the state of the world, such action ensures a smoother adjustment of educational output to educational inputs and improves the chances of market clearance."[39]

37. Harbison and Myers, op. cit, pp. 11-12.

38. Alexander V. Alex 'Human Capital Approach to Economic Development', p. 204.

39. Mark Blaug, "Approaches to Educational Planning', in the book 'Human Capital Formation and Manpower Development' by Wykstra, p. 480.

The discussion on human resource development becomes incomplete, if the population aspects are not looked into. It is worth analysing to know the extent of interdependence between population growth and economic development. The relation of the two is positive in respect of the advanced countries which nourish a fear of secular-stagnation as is advocated by Alvın Havsen. It is the growth of population which opens up opportunities of increasing investment in the developed countries. On the contrary, in the less-developed countries both are inversely related. Population growth is believed to retard the progress of economic development. The economic development in turn is supposed to increase the income which slows down the population growth by reducing the fertility rates. In the wake of economic development, many facilities and forces develop so as to curb the population growth. In developing economies, an increase in population growth is an increase in dependency-ratio and an increase in old-age people both of which drain the income of the productive-age group people. The parting with an income reduces the standard of living of the people in general including those who are working. The lower the standard of living, the lesser is the productivity, the lesser is the productivity, the slower is the augmentation of national output. Secondly, entrepreneurial class does grow commensurately with the growth of population in general. The meagre is the entrepreneurial class, gloomy is the prospect of development. Finally, increased population requires huge amount of investible funds for its upliftment because of its huge size and long gestation period and the limited resources in the developing economies cannot afford to support such population. However, as it is already mentioned, economic development increases income which can be used for creating technical personnel, for financing research programmes, for investing in industries and other physical amenities. All these and other considerations have soothing effect on population. For instance, investment in health measures reduces mortality rates, increases medical facilities and ensures basic as well as minimum needs of the population. Though population grows independent of income, income does breed direct and indirect influences on population and thereby trends in population growth go on turning to be favourable for economic development. Of course, this process is gradual and time-consuming. The people of the less developed countries do not have that much patience, and are not ready to observe austerity measures for sake of posterity. They wish to reach a rapid rate of growth by eliminating evil effects of population in the immediate future. This has caused the adoption of birth-control measures. Population restraint has become regular feature of the less-developed countries.

In this connection, there are two views. Traditional view is that population growth of the world limits the availability of water, food, energy and pure environment, whereas the recent school of thought envisages that by 2000 A.D, economic development softens and smoothens the adverse effects of population growth and the world will be happy. Nevertheless, population planning is the need of our present times so far as India is concerned. It should be made a part and parcel of overall planning. In other words, population planning needs to be integrated with the development planning in general. Integration refers to the explicit consideration of socio-economic and demographic interrelationships in the formulation of development policies and programmes to achieve a country's development goals and objectives.[40] This integration should take place in (a) macro-planning perspective, (b) sectoral planning perspective and (c) programme or project planning perspective.

---

40. p. 51, Asia-Pacific Population Journal, ESCAP, UNO, Vol. I, No. 1, p. 51 March 1986—"Integrating Population and Development Planning" by Alejandro N. Herrin, Henry Pardoko, Tan Boon Ann and Chira Hongladarom, pp. 49-74.

5

Intersectoral Linkages Between Agriculture and Industry

Though each sector has been dealt with separately in the foregoing chapters, it is observed that all sectors are interdependent. No single sector progresses without mutual reinforcement of each other. It is therefore necessary to know the nature and extent of their mutual interdependence. In India, there are some empirical studies made in this connection. Some studies have been able to establish the relationship between agriculture and manufacturing through price-structure of their products. It is true that in exchange economy the prices of agricultural commodities and products influence the prices of manufactured goods and articles and vice versa. Impact of price-changes goes deeper in effecting changes in resource transfer, production and investment decisions in both sectors. Besides, purchasing power of the consumers undergoes changes and incomes of agriculturists and manufacturers also fluctuate. To a certain extent, these domestic price-changes affect the world prices in the international markets and vice versa. These changes in the world prices take place through imports and exports affecting the balance of payments position.

A few studies have been conducted to show how there has been a relationship between agriculture and industry by way of inputs and outputs of the relative sectors. For example, agricultural commodities and products are used as inputs of certain industries. Similarly, some industries supply their output as inputs of agriculture. This sort of mutual dependence has been also illustrated by means of linkage effects. Some other studies have attempted to explain the sectoral interdependence in the form of terms of trade between agricultural commodities and industrial products. There have been a few other empirical studies that go to show the relative contribution to the national income by way of tax-revenue. Of course, there has been very scanty literature to show how far the service-sector has been able to influence agricultural activities and industrial production. Perhaps, this aspect has been kept uncovered due to difficulties of calculation (in quantitative terms) of the services that embody each kind of economic activity in different sectors. Nevertheless, it is quite evident that man is behind any economic activity that takes place either in agriculture or industry. Let us analyse the various empirical studies that have been undertaken to throw some light on the issue of mutual relationship between agricultural and non-agricultural pursuits in India.

Relative prices of agricultural commodities and manufctured goods are useful signs of indicating the trends of resource flow in between these two sectors via domestic terms of trade. "A turn against industry will redress itself if it induces accelerated technological change in agriculture and consequent linkage effects with industry through relaxed wage goods constraint and increased consumer demand. Conversely, a turn against agriculture will redress itself if it encourages accelerated industrial employment growth, consequent greater demand for agricultural wage goods, and increased efficiency of industrial production."[41] It is quite evident that in

41. John W. Mellor "Food Price Policy and Income Distribution in Low Income Countries", Economic Development and Cultural Change, Vol. 27, No. 1, October 1978, pp. 1-26 (op. cit).

less developed countries at least in their initial stages of development agricultural sector supports industrial sector. Rathore, Nadda and Singh have worked out wholesale prices and terms of trade of both the sectors during the period of 1947-48 and 1977-78. Though they have worked out the relative prices and terms of trade on the basis of different base periods, for our analysis the base-period of 1970-71 has been taken out. Of course, the authors admit that different base-periods reflect different turns of terms of trade. If earlier base-periods such as 1952-53=100 and 1961-62=100 are taken, the terms of trade are favourable for the agricultural sector and if the base period of 1970-71=100 is taken the terms of trade are favourable for industrial sector. Since the present study is interested in showing the trends in the relationship between agriculture and industry, the base-period of 1970-71 has been taken for an instance. Table-I shows the details of relative prices and terms of trade between 1947-48 and 1977-78 taking 1970-71 as the base.

Table-I shows that the indices of wholesale prices of food articles have varied from 33.8 in 1947-48 to 173.6 in 1977-78 indicating a rise of about 140 points in the indices of food articles. The corresponding picture of the manufactured articles shows that the indices of manufactured articles went up from 37.5 in 1947-48 to 179.2 in 1977-78 accounting for about 142 points rise in the indices of the manufactured articles. In other words, the trends of change of the price-indices of both food and manufactured articles are in favour of the manufacturing sector. Again, the terms of trade of food articles and manufactured articles show that there has been only an increase of 6.75 points in 1977-78 above the index of 1947-48 in respect of food articles and the corresponding rise in respect of the manufactured articles has been of the order of 8.64 points in 1977-78 above that of 1947-48. From this picture, it can be inferred that agricultural sector has served as reinforcing sector for the industrial sector.

TABLE—I

Indices of Wholesale Prices and Terms of Trade in India
(1970.71=100)

Year	Food Articles	Manufactured articles	Terms of trade
Pre-Plan			
1947-48	33.8	37.2	90.13
First Plan			
1951-52	46.2	51.4	89.88
1955-56	36.1	44.9	80.40
Second Plan			
1956-57	42.0	50.1	83.83
1960-61	48.1	59.5	80.84
Third Plan			
1961-62	48.5	60.2	80.56
1965-66	71.1	74.4	95.56
Annual Plan			
1966 67	82.7	83.4	99.16
1968-69	92.5	92.8	99.68
Fourth Plan			
1969-70	97.5	93.1	104.73
1973-74	136.6	139.5	97.92
Fifth Plan			
1974-75	172.1	168.8	101.95
1977-78	173.6	179.2	96.88

Indian Journal of Agricultural Economics, Vol.34, No.4, p. 69, Conference Number October-December 1979—"Inter-sectoral Terms of Trade in India, 1947-1978" by M.S. Rathore, A.L. Nadda and V.K. Singh.

According to the study made by Rathore, Nadda and Singh, it is observed that percentage change in the per capita expenditure on non-agricultural products has been declining during the period 1956-57 and 1973-74 in respect of both rural and urban areas. Table-11 gives the details that are based on the National Sample Survey findings.

From Table-II it is further noticed that the proportion of expenditure incurred by the rural population on non-agricultural products increased up to 1960-61 and thereafter it declined, whereas the corresponding proportion in urban areas declined continuously from 1956-57 till 1972-74. Total per capita expenditure on both types of products has lower in the rural areas than in the urban areas. Of course, the percentage of the total per capita expenditure on agricultural commodities has been found to be higher than that on non-agricultural products. It means in other words that the consumption pattern of the people in both rural and urban areas has more slant on the consumption of agricultural products which are of course the basic necessities of living. Though this is true in most cases, the percentage rise in the per capita expenditure on agricultural products in urban areas has gone up from 44.49% in 1956-57 to 59.11% in 1973-74 which is a steeper rise than its corresponding rise in respect of rural areas that, works out to be from 65.74% in 1956-57 to 67.82% in 1973-74. In the rural areas, the predominance of agricultural products in their per capita expenditure has maintained more or less the similar trend. In urban areas also, the higher trend in the proportion of per capita expenditure on agricultural products over the years is meaningful. This serves as an indicator of expanding demand for the agricultural products in urban areas and it is a market-stimulus for agriculture to augment its production.

The inter-industry transactions have been studied by N.V. Namboodir[42] and thereby linkage effects have also been worked out. Agriculture supplies vital inupts to industry and vice versa. It is observed that the dependence of the manufacturing sector on agriculture is heavier than the dependence of agriculture on manufacturing sector. Table-III illustrates this point.

42. ibid, p. 91-97. The Production Linkage Between Agriculture and the Manufacturing Sector" by N.V. Namboodiri.

TABLE—II

Per capita Expenditure on Agricultural and Non-Agricultural Products for Final Use in Rural and Urban Areas According to The Various Rounds of The National Sample Survey : All-India

(Rs.)

Rounds of N.S.S.	Rural Expenditure on :			Urban Expenditure on :		
	Agricultural Products	Non-Agricultural Products	Total expenditure	Agricultural Products	Non-Agricultural Products	Total expenditure
11th Round (1956-57)	11.11 (65.74)	5.80 (38.18)	16.97	11.15 (44.49)	10.95 (43.70)	25.06
16th Round (1960-61)	13.33 (62.09)	8.08 (37.63)	21.47	15.91 (53.90)	12.38 (41.94)	29.52
21st Round (1966-67)	20.55 (66.50)	10.29 (33.30)	30.90	22.84 (54.98)	16.92 (40.73)	41.54
25th Round (1970-71)	23.52 (66.61	11.72 (33.19)	35.31	30.01 (56.78)	20.26 (38.33)	52.85
28th Round (1973-74)	35.95 (67.82)	17.00 (32.07)	53.01	41.83 (59.11)	26.37 (38.33)	70.77
Per cent change	2.22	—6.17	212.37	32.86	—14.74	182.40

Figures in parentheses indicate percentages to total expenditure.

Source : ibid, p. 74.

TABLE—III

Percentage Distribution of Inputs

Sector	Agriculture	Manufacturing	Others	Total Intermediate Use
Agriculture	41.7	20.0	23.8	24.7
Manufacturing	17.5	38.1	51.0	39.8
Others	40.8	41.9	25.2	35.5
Total Input	100.0	100.0	100.0	100.0

The structure of inputs in agriculture reveals that agriculture has used about 42 per cent of the inputs generated by itself and the manufacturing sector has provided about 17.5 per cent and the rest from 'others'. The manufacturing sector has used its own output accounting for 38% and agriculture has provided to the extent of 29 per cent. It is significant to note that of the total share by the 'others' animal husbandry contributed more to the output structure and attracted more from the input structure. "In value terms the input going to agriculture from manufacturing is approximately one-fourth of the value of agricultural output going to manufacture."[43]

For the purpose of comparative analysis, it is interesting to quote another study made in this context by Siegfried Schultz and Dieter Schumacher[44]. Table-IV for example furnishes the details of relationship between agriculture and manufacturing sectors.

43. ibid, p. 92.

44. ECONOMICS, Vol. 19 pp. 34, 57, edited by the Institute for Scientific Cooperation, Tubingen, Federal Republic of Germany 1979—"Inter-industrial Linkages In Developing Economies" by S. Schultz and D. Schumacher.

TABLE—IV

Indicators of the Relationship Between Agriculture and Manufacturing: (Percentages)

	Argentina		Zambia		Rep. of Korea	
	1960	1970	1965	1969	1960	1970
Share of intermediate inputs in total inputs of Agriculture.	37.1	39.1	4.7	13.6	16.5	26.3
Share of manufacturing inputs in total inputs of Agriculture.	4.2	9.5	1.0	5.6	5.7	10.3
Share of manufacturing inputs in total intermediate inputs of agriculture.	11.4	24.3	20.3	40.7	34.4	39.4
Share of intermediate deliveries in total output of manufacturing.	1.1	2.1	0.5	2.0	5.0	5.4
Share of deliveries to agriculture in total output of manufacturing.	2.9	5.1	1.5	4.8	11.4	11.3
Share of deliveries to agriculture in total intermediate deliveries of manufacturing.	62.1	59,6	29.9	35.6	51.5	46.3

Share of intermediate inputs in total inputs of manufacturing.	13.0	9.0	9.7	5.6	11.7	6.9
Share of agricultural inputs in total inputs of manufacturing.	21.0	15.0	29.2	15.6	22.7	14.7
Share of agricultural inputs in total intermediate inputs of manufacturing.	61.1	48.2	16.4	19.0	22.7	27.9
Share of intermediate deliveries in total output of agriculture.	36.5	40.6	33.8	42.8	43.8	47.7
Share of deliveries to manufacturing in total output of agriculture.	51.0	41.3	16.1	5.2	13.3	13.3
Share of deliveries to manufacturing in total intermediate deliveries.	83.4	85.7	98.0	80.0	58.5	47.6

In the case of three developing countries such as Argentina, Zambia and Republic of Korea, Table, IV shows that the importance of manufacturing industries as suppliers of intermediate goods to agriculture increased during the period between 1960 and 1970. The reasons behind this are the increasing intermediate input intensity of agricultural production and a higher share of manufacturing products in total intermediate inputs of agriculture. Thereby, agriculture grew in importance as a buyer also from the point of view of the manufacturing industries. On the other hand, the importance of agricultural products within the intermediate inputs of manufacturing shows a significantly decreasing tendency. This is due to a higher growth of industries outside the processing of agricultural goods. Thus, the deliveries of agricultural products to manufacturing decreased also in relation to total output or to total intermediate deliveries of agriculture. Regarding the total relations between agriculture and manufacturing it can be stated : "On the one hand, the growing intensity of the use of manufactured goods in agriculture will induce increased production stimuli for manufacturing industries when the agricultural production capacities enlarged. On the other hand, the flow of agricultural products to manufacturing will lose importance from the point of view of both manufacturing and agriculture."[45] The comparative analysis of the study of Namboodiri and that of Schultz and Schumacher indicates that in India manufacturing sector covers processing industries whereas in case of Argentina, Zambia and Republic of Korea processing sector has been crossed by the manufacturing sector. Hence, the role of agriculture in the industrialization of India appears to be more significant and influential than that in the case of industrialization in the latter countries. Nevertheless, it has been proved by both studies that there has been a good deal of relationship between agriculture and industry.

Further, it seems to be more meaningful if the linkage effects are studied. According to Namboodiri's study, backward linkage of agriculture is very weak. Table-V gives the clear idea of backward linkage and forward linkage in between agriculture and industry.

45. ibid. 45. pp. 56-57,

TABLE—V

Linkage Between Agriculture And The Manufacturing Sector

Particulars	Food Crops	Cash Crops	Plantation Crops.	Others	Total
I. Backward linkage from agriculture (i.e. manufacturing Sector forward linkage) :-					
a) Total purchase of agriculture from manufacturing sector as a percentage of :					
1) Total output of manufacturing sector.	2.35	0.47	0.10	0.84	3.76
2) Total agricultural input.	15.00	17.31	76.08	28.32	17.50
b) Linkage co-efficient.	0.2476	0.1469	0.0417	0.0882	0.1813
II. Agriculture's forward linkage (i.e. backward linkage from manufacturing sector) :					
a) Total intermediate sale of agriculture to manufacturing sector as a percentage of :					
1) Total agricultural output**	1.16	50.60	40.80	6.67	11.52
2) Total input of manufacturing sector.	0.74	9.48	1.26	2.17	13.65
(b) Linkage co-efficient.	0.1934	1.3188	0.6893	0.6594	0.4271

* Total input used by respective crops.

** Total output value of respective crops.

Source : Indian Journal of Agricultural Economics, Vol. 34, No. 4, October-December 1976.

From Table -V it is evident that agriculture supplies its products for manufacturing sector to the tune of 13.65 per cent of the total input of manufacturing sector, and 11.52 per cent of its total output. These percentages vary form one branch of agriculture to another. For instance, in the case of food crops, these percentages are 0.74 and 1.16 respectively and in respect of cash crops they are 9.48 and 50.6 respectively. The plantation crops exhibit these percentages amounting to 1.26 and 40.80 respectively. Similarly, agriculture's backward linkage varies from one branch of agriculture to the another. For instance, total purchase of agriculture from manufacturing sector accounts for 15 per cent of total inputs of the food crops, 17.3 per cent of the total inputs of cash crops, 76.8 per cent of total inputs of plantation crops and 28.32 per cent of total inputs of other crops in agricultural sector. The purchase of agriculture ftom manufacturing sector, again varies from 2.35 per cent of the total output of manufacturing sector required by the food crops to 0.47 per cent and 0.10 per cent and 0.84 per cent of total output of manufacturing sector required by cash crops, plantation crops and other crops respectively. Backward linkage coefficient of agriculture is high in case of food crops being 0.2476 as compared to other crops, whereas forward linkage of agriculture in respect of 'food crops has low coefficient being 0.1834 as against forward linkage coefficient of cash crops being 1.3188. Forward linkage coefficients of plantation crops and other crops in agricultural sector are 0.6893 and 0.6594 respectively. Namboodiri has however opined that a stronger production linkage is important for the development of both agriculture and manufacturing. As a result of the increased demand for new inputs in agriculture, there would have been a positive change in the agriculture's backward linkage. A better production linkage could be attained through : (1) broad-based diffusion of new agriculture technology, (ii) creating demand for processed food, (iii) larger investments on social overheads such as irrigation, electricity, etc., and (iv) discouraging the export of primary agricutural products, etc.[46]

46. Namboodiri, op. cit. p. 97,

Schultz and Schumacher also have worked out the linkages of twenty sectors in their study of inter industrial linkages in developing countries.[47] On the basis of this study Table-VI has been prepared.

From Table VI it is evident that in India backward linkage of agriculture, forestry and fishing is higher (21 per cent) than the total average (17 per cent) for Latin America, Africa and Asia taken together. If individual countries in Asia are studied, the backward linkages of agricultural sector in Philippines and Republic of Korea are higher being 33 per cent and 26 per cent respectively than that of India.[48] The forward linkage of agriculture, forestry and fishing in India is higher (44 per cent) than the total average (35 per cent for Latin America, Africa and Asia put together. Of course, the average forward linkage of agricultural sector in India is lower than the total average for Asia (45 per cent) as a whole. If individual countries in Asia are taken, India stands sixth in ranking as per the forward linkage. The highest forward linkage of agricultural sector is found in Malaysia (W) being 61 per cent followed by that of Pakistan (57 per cent).

For financing of economic development, it is necessary to ascertain to what extent agriculture and industry contribute revenue by way of taxes to the country's exchequer. From the point of intersectoral equity it is useful and interesting to find out the contributions of both sectors towards public revenue. It is also important to locate the sources of investible surplus for financing economic development by means of relative ability to pay the taxes of agriculture and industry. Table-VII gives the break down of relative shares of tax contribution to both sectors during the period 1951-52 and 1968-69.

---

47. S. Schultz & D. Schumacher, op. cit. pp. 43-44.

48. For details see Tables III & IV, ibid,

TABLE—VI

Cross-Section Of Indicator Values In Absolute Terms (Percentage) (1960 to 1970)

Standard Sectors	Backward Linkages (Average)					Forward Linkages (Average)				
	Latin America	Africa	Asia	India	Total Average	Latin America	Africa	Asia	India	Total Average
1. Agriculture, forestry and fishing.	19	12	19	21	17	31	23	45	44	35
2. Apparel, Ind. Textiles and footwear.	28	23	21	13	23	57	07	57	94	39
3. Processed foods.	62	55	62	30	59	17	11	16	19	14
4. Apparel, Ind. Textiles & footwear.	56	37	39	57	41	28	15	25	30	22
5. Leather & Leather Products.	57	52	50	48	52	58	6	35	39	30
6. Wood & Paper Production, Printing.	51	35	44	19	42	63	52	63	55	59
7. Rubber Products.	28	31	50	57	41	63	37	54	60	52

8.	Chemicals.	40	35	38	39	37	49	30	48	60	42
9.	Petroleum Products.	44	17	29	61	32	81	28	71	55	68
10.	Non-metallic Mineral Products.	46	49	44	25	46	84	77	91	77	87
11.	Basic metals, metal Products.	51	29	42	37	40	68	61	55	67	59
12.	Non-electrical Machinery	32	32	26	32	29	43	70	39	6	47
13.	Electrical Machinery	42	11	3'	39	34	37	52	43	7	42
14.	Transport Equipment.	28	23	34	36	31	39	77	30	30	44
15.	Industry, n.e.c.	38	29	34	—	33	18	42	19	—	26
16.	Electricity, gas, water.	26	22	29	14	26	57	66	51	67	58
17.	Construction.	49	38	48	39	45	4	20	5	—	10
18.	Trade.	12	26	14	—	18	23	45	32	—	36
19.	Transport, storage and communications.	33	29	26	19	27	29	49	39	—	42
20.	Services.	11	24	16	—	18	21	25	16	—	20

TABLE—VII

Tax Incidence And Average Tax Rates (1951-52 to 1968-69) In India

Year	Tax Incidence: Agricultural Sector (Rs. crores)	Tax Incidence: Non-Agricultural Sector (Rs. crores)	Average Tax Rates: Agricultural Sector: Taxes per capita (Rs.)	Average Tax Rates: Agricultural Sector: Ratio of Taxes to per capita Income	Average Tax Rates: Non-Agricultural Sector: Taxes per capita (Rs.)	Average Tax Rates: Non-Agricultural Sector: Ratio of Taxes to P.C.
1951-52	200	450	8	3.8	41.8	9.5
1960-61	399	922	13.4	5.6	68.9	13.0
1968-69	907	2693	26.4	6.5	174.0	19.1

Sources: Indian Journal of Agricultural Economics, Conference Issue, October-December 1979-p. 115, "Inter-Sectoral Linkages—Flow of Surplus For Financing Investment", by M.M. Batra.

It is seen in Table-VII that tax incidence in terms of revenue to the State exchequer has been more on non-agricultural sector over the years concerned. For instance, in 1951-52 agricultural sector contributed Rs. 200 crores which went up to Rs.907 crores in 1968-69, whereas non-agricultural sectors contributed Rs. 450 crores in 1951-52 which went up to Rs. 2693 crores in 1968-69. The ratio of total tax incidence on agricultural sector to that on non-agricultural sector works out to be 4.9 in 1951-52 as against 1:3 in 1968-69. Even from the point of average tax rate, taxes per capita in agricultural sector are lower (i.e. Rs.8, Rs.13.4 and Rs.26.4 in 1951-52, 1960-61 and 1968-69 respectively). The ratio of taxes to per capita income in agricultural sector works out to be 3.8, 5.6 and 6.5 in 1951-52, 1960-61 and 1968-69 respectively, whereas the corresponding ratios in non-agricultural sector are 9.5, 13.0 and 19.1 respectively in the crorresponding years. Of course, per capita taxes on incomes have increased in both sectors over the years concerned. Mr. Batra has observed in this context as following: "A rational taxation policy for the developing economy must evolve a proper policy for optimum tapping of the taxable capacity which is continuously on the increase. The growing productivity of the rural sector if siphoned off effectively through taxation will not only discourage wasteful expenditure among the rural masses but could also provide ample funds for investment in non-agricultural sector. Besides, it will tend to reduce the growing tendencies to hoard the marketable surplus of agricultural crops.[49] Intersectoral equity demands that the agriculturists, particularly the big farmers, who have achieved significant increases in income should provide for investible surplus for financing development in both the agricultural and non-agricultural sectors. Garg, Singh, Azad and Tewari have concluded in their article "Agricultural and Industrial Development and Their Interdependence in India" that the further growth in agricultural production in India is materially dependent on the rapid increase in the production of inputs supplying industries. This will help in the use of modern technology in agricultural production. Similarly, the rapid growth of industries is basically dependent on the development of agricultural production, particularly of the raw materials used by the industries.[50]

Some studies[51] on factor shares in Indian agriculture also reveal that the linkages between farm and non-farm activities have increased in India in recent times (See Table—VIII).

From the Table-VIII, it is evident that the share of inputs in the gross value of output has increased significantly during the seventies and this is much more so in the case of technological advanced regions. It is an indication of the growing

49. ibid, P.119.
50. ibid, P.127.
51. Indian Journal of Agrieultural Economics, July-September, 1983 p. 401.

TABLE—VIII

Factor Proportions In The Gross Value of Output (Per cent)

Crop/State	Triennium	Wages	Rent	Interest	Surplus	Total value added	Inter-mediate input
Paddy:	1957-60	21.37	49.29	0.01	– 5.49	65.19	34.82
Andhra Pradesh	1967-70	18.25	34.75	6.61	1.63	61.84	38.16
	1978-79	22.90	27.90	6.90	1.40	59.10	40.90
West Bengal	1971-74	21.70	24.50	2.60	30.00	78.80	21.20
	1978-81	32.80	24.30	5.40	4.30	66.80	32.20
Orissa	1971-74	22.10	24.90	3.30	25.60	75.90	24.10
	1978-81	26.30	24.70	5.00	16.70	72.70	27.30
Wheat:							
Punjab	1967-70	21.0	16.90	3.40	30.60	71.90	28.10
	1978-81	13.80	25.90	8.40	8.60	56.70	43.30
Uttar Pradesh	1971-74	14.20	23.00	4.40	26.60	67.20	32.80
	1978-81	15.70	21.20	7.00	7.10	63.00	37.00

Source: Indian Journal of Agricultural Economics, July-September, 1983, p. 401.

linkages of modern agriculture on the non-farm sector. Increase in the share of capital has also been substantial. This has resulted from increased investment in fixed capital as well as more intensive use of purchased inputs consequent to the adoption of new technology.

In conclusion, it seems appropriate to summarize the relationship between agriculture and industry in India in the words of Hans-Bernd Schafer [52]: The role played by agriculture in the industrialization of the third world can scarcely be exaggerated. It must feed the non-agricultural population. It must supply the work-force for the modern sector, under circumstances in which the work-force needed grows too quickly to keep pace with the national growth of population. Lastly, it acts as a market for industrial consumer goods, products for further processing and capital goods. Its first task, to supply the industrial work-force and to provide the food and textile industries with their material, is often placed in the foreground. This is particularly the case in countries which are attempting to break free from world trade by means of a strategy of import substitution, and whose industrial sector fails to earn enough foreign currency to ensure the feeding of the urban population from imports. This is also true, however, for large countries, whose foreign trade is only a relatively small proportion of their total trade.

In this regard considerable importance is attached once again to agricultural price levels, as compared with the price level of industrial goods, the intersectoral terms of trade. If agricultural prices are very high, then because of the high proportion of agricultural products in the consumption of the average household, wages—expressed in terms of industrial goods—and thereby the unit costs of industrial production must be relatively high. The margin for profits, industrial investment and growth is thus correspondingly narrow. On the other hand, if agricultural prices are too low, farmers

52. ECONOMICS, edited by The Institute for Scientific Cooperation, Tubingen, Federal Republic of Germany 1982 PP. 48-49, "The Exchange Relationship Between Industry And Agriculture And The Stagnation of Industry in India" by Hans-Bernd Schafer.

lose the incentive to produce or to offer for sale agricultural products in sufficient quantities. There then arises the danger of a crisis in supplying the towns, with serious political consequences. Even so, the attempt was often made—as in the case of mercantilism—to keep down food prices in the cities by administrative means, for fear of social unrest, but above all for reasons of industrialization. Production for the market, which was thereby set at risk, was maintained very often by compulsion and force. High taxes on agriculture in Japan in the 19th century and forcible collectivization in the Soviet Union in the 1930s were both imposed in order that industrial potential should not be stunted because of insufficient development of the agricultural surplus.

However, there are examples of industrialization being hindered by a swifter and more sustained rise in agricultural prices, as a result of which a country finds itself in the terms-of-trade trap of industrial stagnation. One of these examples is India whose industrial sector entered a period of severe crisis in the 1960s, after a period of successful development.

6

International Trade in Agricultural Commodities and Total World Trade

Agriculture, among other contributions to economic development, earns foreign exchange which is critically required by the most of the developing countries. Some economists argue that in the early stages of development of developing economies international trade in agricultural commodities does not influence the overall domestic activities of the countries concerned. This is perhaps due to the fact that the proportion of total trade of developing economies in agricultural products forms negligible part of the total world trade. Though this argument is true to a certain extent, the developing economies cannot afford to neglect their international trade relations. At present, such countries are not closed economies, they are for all practical purposes open ones. Hla Myint has studied this, problem in relation to the ideas of 'closed economy', 'semi-open economy' and 'open economy' and has concluded that agriculture earns foreign exchange through trading in agricultural commodities, among others, in international markets. "—by means of appropriate agricultural development policies the agricultural sector can be made to increase its contribution[53] to the foreign exchange supply————". Further, it is observed that international trade in agricultural commodities plays an important role so as to influence the international prices. "In an open economy, the terms of trade between industrial goods and food can be stabilized by international prices.————with elastic demand for exports and supplies of imports and provided spending is no greater than output, sectoral balance is easily achieved by foreign trade".[54]

Primary products are a major source of foreign reserves for less developed countries. Name a country in Latin America, Africa or Asia, one or a few principal primary product exports can be associated with it. In both Chile and Zambia, copper counts for about two-thirds of total exports. In Egypt cotton is slightly less than half of total exports. In Bangla desh it is jute, in Malaysia and Bolivia tin, in Thailand rice, rubber and tin. For 10 Latin American countries coffee is the first or second export product. Proportions are lower in some other countries, and several (such as Peru) divide their exports among several products. Naturally, amounts and percentages vary from year to year. Only in a very few LDCs (such as India) are manufactures approaching a substantial proportion of exports.[55]

It is quite evident from the above paragraphs that no country can afford to neglect international trade whether it be in manufactured goods or in the primary products. Of course, the impact of trade is to be measured by the nature of terms of trade. If the terms of trade are favourable for a particular country, its national income will be enhanced, it will be able to obtain additional financial resources for financing its development, it increases the welfare of its people from gains from trade and it

53 Agriculture in Development Theory edited by Lloyd G. Reynolds, Chapter 12, p. 338, "Agriculture and Economic Development in the open economy" by Hla Myint

54. Economic Development, (2nd edition) by C.P. Kindleberger Chapter 12, p. 215, "Industrialization versus Agriculture".

55. Economic Impact, No. 22, Quarterly Review of World Economics p. 33-34, — "The LDCs and the Terms of Trade," by Powelson.

allocates productive resources in an optimum manner in between different sectors of its economy, preferable more in the export-oriented sectors. On the other hand, if the terms of trade are unfavourable, the opposite will be the effects. As a result, it becomes inevitable on the part of each trading country to see that its terms of trade must be favourable for itself.

Since the terms of trade of many of the developing economies fluctuate widely from time to time, there comes the role of international commodity arrangements. The main objectives of these trade agreements are : (1) to ensure demand for and, supply of particular commodity for which agreement has been done; and (2) to avoid price-fluctuations of the commodities that enter into agreement. Though these arrangements appear to be apparently useful for the developing economies, they do not help in expanding the quantum of international trade in general. Besides, these agreements serve very limited purposes of the countries concerned. "The agree ments operated in post-war years have succeeded in serving some limited objectives, but they have not proved capable of dealing with the two main sets of commodity problems that call for action; the need for some assurances, particularly to low-income exporting countries, of fairly stable and remunerative average levels of export-proceeds for a number of years ahead, say for the five-year periods normally covered by national development plans; and the need for improved international coordination of national policies of the developed countries."[56]

The significance of international trade in primary (agricultural) commodities is also seen by assessing the expansion of world trade in agricultural commodities in proportion to the growth of world trade in manufactured goods and by ascertaining the share of the primary producing countries in the total world trade of all commodities and particularly in the primary products. Prof. Dantwala has summarised

56. Problems In Economic Development, [edited by E.A.G. Robinson, Chapter 33: p. 561, "International Commodity Arrangements" by Dr. Greda Blau.

these trends during the period from 1920s till 1960s as below :

"(1) World trade in primary products is not expanding proportionately in the manufacturing output. The index of manufacturing production with 1928 as the base was 246 in 1955-57 while the index of exports of primary commodities was no more than 132; the index of exports of manufactures stood at 203....A variety of factors account for the sluggishness in trade in primary commodities. Apart from the income-elasticity effect the sluggishness may be due to (i) domestic supplies replacing imports, (ii) raw material saving technology and shifts in composition of manufactures production, (iii) growth of synthetic substitutes and better utilization of scraps, and (iv) supply deficiencies.

"(2) The share of the primary producing countries in the total trade as well as the trade in the primary products has been more or less stagnant since 1938 and declining since 1948. In other words, the industrial areas are becoming increasingly self-sufficient. As Nurkse put it : 'They are becoming each other's best customers'. In 1960 almost 50 per cent of the import requirements of the industrial areas for primary products were supplied by the industrial areas themselves."

"(3) Import demand of the primary producing countries, on the other hand, has been growing and appears to be price inelastic. This imbalance between the export earnings and import requirements has been clearly reflected in the growing balance of trade and payment deficits of the non-industrial areas and their sinking foreign exchange resources." Prof. Dantwala has shown in his paper that the deterioration in terms of trade of primary commodities during the 1950s and particularly since 1954 is not disputed. However, the export prospects of primary commodities from the developing countries depend on (i) to what extent there would be demand for primary products from the industrial countries, (ii) how much the developing countries could afford to export outside their economies, (iii) how far the less developed countries would be demanding the capital goods and other maintenance material from the advanced countries,[57] and (iv) the nature and quantum of supply of primary products from the developed countries to the international markets.

The demand for primary products from the developed countries appears not to increase in future because of low income elasticity of demand and emergence of synthetic substitutes for food products. The rise in domestic demand for agricultural commodities due to rise in population is perhaps met by the rise in their agricultural productivity. Even the developing economies seem to be averse to the increased exports because their increased population requires increased agricultural production including food articles. The agricultural productivity in those economies also does not rise in proportionate manner as the rise in population. Though the developing countries need more and more import of capital goods and other maintenance raw materials, these countries tend to resort to import...substituting measures. As a result, export component of these countries in terms of primary goods may not increase. The developed countries in turn afford to supply more of their primary products in the international markets due to their progressive and commercialized agriculture. As such, the exports of primary products from the developing countries face severe competition and thereby the exports of the latter tend to decline in the international markets due to their high cost of production and inferiority of their quality. In brief, there appears to be future for the exports of primary products and the result would be a decline in their participation in the total world trade as well as in the world trade of agricultural commodities. The increased exports of agricultural commodities from the developed countries tend to increase in the international markets but the relative growth of exports of manufactured goods happens to be greater than that of primary exports resulting in the decline of the proportion of trade in primary products in the total world trade as a whole.

---

57. Ibid, pp.499-500, "Commodity Terms of Trade of Primary Producing Countries" by M.L. Dantwala.

"Historically, the prices of primary commodities (the exports of most LDCs) have declined relative to manufactured goods (the principal exports of developed nations). As a result, the terms of trade have on the average tended to worsen for Third World countries (excluding the major oil producers during the 1970s) while they improved for the developed countries. For example, between 1955 and 1970 the terms of trade for developed countries rose by over 10 per cent while those of the Third World fell by over 7 per cent. The LDCs therefore had to sell greater and greater quantities of their primary products (the international demand for which is relatively income inelastic) in order to purchase a given quantity of manufactured imports. One estimate placed the extra costs of deteriorating terms of trade for the LDCs at over $2.5 billion per year during the last decade. Much of the argument against primary product export expansion and in favour of diversification into manufactured exports for the Third World countries during the 1950s and 1960s was based on this secular deterioration of their commodity terms of trade".[58]

Composition and Quantum of World Trade in Primary Commodities

The interrelationship between primary commodities and the manufactured goods is vivid when 70 per cent of the exports from LDCs consist of the primary commodities while 76 per cent of the exports from the advanced countries comprise non-primary products. Even at present the same picture holds good without much change in the composition of exports (See Table IX & IXA).

In spite of the predominance of primary commodities in the exports of the less developed countries, the total quantum of such goods does not keep pace with rise in the world trade taken as a whole. On the other hand, over the three decades which ended in 1980, per capita food production and per capita agricultural production (which includes not only food

58. Economics for a Developing World, by M.P Todaro, 1977, p. 297.

TABLE—IX

Structure of World Exports, 1970, 1975 and 1979 (Percentage) By Destination.

	World	Developed Market Economies	Developing Countries & Territories	Socialist Countries of Eastern Europe.	Socialist Countries of Asia
All Products:					
1970	100	70.5	18.7	9.2	0.9
1975	100	65.7	23.0	9.5	1.0
1979	100	68.4	22.3	7.8	1.1
All Food Items:					
1970	100	72.6	17.7	8.3	1.0
1975	100	65.8	22.5	10.1	0.8
1979	100	66.2	22.0	9.8	1.4
Agricultural Raw Materials:					
1970	100	74.1	13.5	10.8	1.4
1975	100	71.5	15.9	10.2	2.1
1979	100	72.8	16.8	7.9	2.5
Ores & Metals:					
1970	100	76.1	11.9	9.8	1.5
1975	100	63.1	19.8	13.8	2.3
1979	100	66.9	18.9	11.2	2.8
Fuels:					
1970	100	73.6	16.2	9.8	0.4
1975	100	73.9	17.2	4.5	0.1
1979	100	75.9	16.9	4.8	0.1
Manufactured Goods:					
1970	100	68.6	20.8	9.3	0.8
1975	100	62.7	25.7	10.1	1.0
1979	100	66.4	24.5	7.9	0.9

Hand Book of International Trade and Development Statistics, 1981 Supplement, U.N.O, p.80.

TABLE—IX A

Structure of World Imports, 1970, 1975 and 1979 (Percentage Shows by Origin)

	World	Developed Market Economies	Developing Countries & Territories	Socialist Countries of Eastern Europe	Socialist Countries of Asia.
All products:					
1970	100	71.9	17.6	9.8	0.7
1975	100	66.1	24.2	8.9	0.8
1979	100	65.4	25.4	8.2	0.9
All Food Items:					
1970	100	59.0	32.1	7.3	1.6
1975	100	63.1	28.9	6.0	2.0
1979	100	63.2	29.8	4.8	2.1
Agricultural Raw Materials:					
1970	100	58.3	30.4	9.6	1.6
1975	100	62.2	25.0	11.1	1.7
1979	100	60.5	28.6	8.8	2.2
Ores & Metals:					
1970	100	70.1	18.7	10.6	0.6
1975	100	74.2	14.7	10.4	0.7
1979	100	74.8	15.6	8.8	0.7
Fuels:					
1970	100	26.5	63.2	10.2	0.1
1915	100	17.3	74.1	8.2	0.5
1979	100	18.9	70.9	9.8	0.5
Manufactured Goods:					
1970	100	85.2	5.2	9.1	0.6
1975	100	84.1	6.7	8.6	0·6
1979	100	82.6	9.1	7.5	0.8

Ibid, p. 821.

but also non-edible agricultural products like cotton, sisal, rubber, etc.) each increased less than one per cent per year in the Third World as a whole (Table-X). Moreover, the rates of growth of both these measures of agricultural performance were much slower in LDCs than those in developed countries. People on the whole were little or no better off in terms of the per capita availability of food at the end of 1980 than they were at the beginning. In contrast, in the more developed countries, per capita food production continued to rise.

TABLE—X

The Growth of Percapita Agricultural Production and Percapita Food Production (Growth Rates : 1969-71=100)

	Per Capita Agricultural Production		Per Capita Food Production	
	1967-80	1967-80	1967-80	1970-80
World	0.5	0.5	0.6	0.7
Developed Market Economies	1.0	1.2	1.0	1.3
Developing Countries and Territories	0.7	0.8	0.9	0.9
Socialist Countries Eastern Europe	1.1	1.0	1.1	0.9
Socialist Countries Asia	1.6	1.7	1.7	1.7

Source: Hand Book of International Trade and Development Statistics, 1981, Supplement, U.N.O., p. 360 & 361.

The 1970s also witnessed the transition from a previous era of commercial food surpluses to one of global shortages, rising prices and growing national concern primarily among the least developed of Third World Countries. While droughts in parts of Africa and Asia exacerbated the short-term seriousness of the world food-problem, its long-term trend has been in the direction of a narrowing gap between total world production and world consumption. Food prices are likely to remain much higher than they were during the previous decade and, one continent, North America is emerging as only major world source of exportable food supplies. Almost half of the World's population will continue to be overwhelmingly dependent on North American food supplies. But rising prices of petroleum and fertilizers, major imports of most poor countries, greatly deplete those foreign exchange funds that would ordinarily be used to buy food from these large grain suppliers.

In the second development decade (1970-1980), the world trade as a whole stagnated. But the average annual rate of change in volume in the agricultural exports has shown some improvement from 4 per cent in 1963-73 to 4½ per cent in 1973-81, whereas the corresponding change of exports of manufactures had declined from 11 per cent in 1963-73 to 5 per cent in 1973-81. In spite of this, in 1981, the average annual rate of change in value in agricultural exports is 3 per cent as against 4½ per cent of the manufactures showing that the rate of expansion of agricultural exports is less than that of the exports of the manufactures (See Table XI).

TABLE—XI

Growth of World Exports, 1963-81 (Average Annual Rate of Change in Volume, Percentage)

	1963-73	1973-81	1974	1975	1976	1977	1978	1979	1980	1981
Total	8½	3½	3½	-3	11	4½	5½	5½	1½	0
Agricultural Products.	4	4½	-3½	5	9½	2	9	7	3	3
Minerals*	7	-2½	-2½	7½	4½	2	1½	5	-8	-12
Manufactures	11	5	8½	-4½	13	5	5	5	4½	4½

*Including fuels and non-ferrous metals.

Source : International Trade, 1981-82, GATT, Geneva, 1982 p.3.

Note : Thus 1981 is the fourth post war year in which the volume of World Trade failed to expand ; the other years are 1952 (down by 2 per cent), 1958 (by 1 per cent) and 1975 (by 3 per cent).

The development of world exports and production in terms of value and volume is seen in Table—XII. The total value of the world exports went up from $ 154 billion in 1963 to $ 1970 in 1981 ($ 5 billion decline as compared to 1980). This trend in the second half of the decade 1970-80 has been definitely higher than that during the 1st half. Similar trend has been noticed in reepect of exports of agricultural exports as well as the exports of the manufactures. In terms of unit value, the total word trade has experienced a rise of above four-fold in 1981 as compared to 1963. For example, index of the whole trade in unit value has increased from 100 in 1963 to 420 in 1981, though there has been a decline of 4 points in 1981 in relation to the previous year 1980. The index of the exports of agricultural products has increased from 100 in 1963 to 315 in 1981, while the corresponding index of the exports of manufactures has increased from 100 in 1963 to 325 in 1981. Thus, in terms of unit value, there has been increase of the world exports in respect of all commodities. In terms of volume, it is clear from Table—XII that the exports of agricultural products have increased about threefold in 1981 taking 1963 as base year whereas the exports of the manufactures have increased more than four-fold in 1981 indicating that the rate of growth of exports of the agricultural products is less than that of the exports of the manufactures. Even in respect of the total production of agricultural products over the period 1963-1981, the rise is about 1½ times as against the corresponding rise of 2½ times in respect of the production of the manufactures.

TABLE—XII

Development of World Exports and Production, 1963, 1973-81.

	1963	1973	1974	1975	1976	1977	1978	1979	1980	1981
World Exports										
Value (billion dollars) Total	154	574	836	873	991	1125	1303	1635	1985	1970
Agricultural Products.	45	121	148	150	166	188	213	262	297	290
Minerals*	26	96	215	207	241	266	276	400	565	540
Manufactures	82	347	459	501	566	648	788	945	1095	1105
Unit Value (1963=100) Total	100	161	227	244	249	271	297	354	424	420
Agricultural Products	100	185	235	225	230	255	262	300	330	315
Minerals*	100	192	445	460	510	550	563	780	1200	1320
Manufactures	100	152	185	212	212	232	266	303	337	325
Volume (1963=100)										
Total	100	231	239	232	258	269	284	300	305	305
Agricultural Products	100	147	142	149	163	166	183	196	202	208

Minerals*	100	195	190	176	184	188	193	201	183	162
Manufactures	100	280	304	290	328	344	364	382	398	416
World Commodity Output Volume (1963=100)										
All Commodities	100	180	185	183	196	205	214	220	223	226
Agriculture	100	128	130	134	137	139	145	147	148	153
Mining	100	171	174	171	181	191	190	199	195	189
Manufacturing	100	197	203	200	216	227	238	249	251	254

* including fuels and non-ferrous metals.

Source: Table AI. Appendices, International Trade, 1981-82, GATT, Geneva 1982.

TABLE—XIII

World Trade In Food Products, 1970-1980 : (Volume Indices & Trends) 1969-71=100

Country Group	Exports				Imports			
	Growth Trend (a)	1978	1979	1980	Growth Trend (b)	1978	1979	1980
World	4.7	148	156	167	4.6	146	157	167
Developed Market Economies	6.3	172	183	204	2.5	127	131	130
North America	7.6	205	212	239	0.8	113	115	109
Developing Countries	2.6	125	128	127	8.6	192	205	245
Africa	-3.5	81	75	78	8.8	210	213	245
Latin America	3.7	140	142	134	9.1	202	208	268
Near East	3.0	143	119	132	13.4	273	300	368
Far East	5.6	146	166	169	4.7	135	151	166
Centrally Planned Economies.	-0.3	90	97	96	7.5	185	227	249
Asia	-0.2	100	111	113	6.9	174	225	249
Eastern Europe and the U.S.S.R.	-0.5	87	93	91	7.7	188	228	256

Source : World Economic Survey, 1981-1982, U.N.O, p. 45.

(a) Excluding fish.

(b) Average annual growth rate 1970-1980.

In particular, the world trade in food products according to regional groupings (Table—XIII) indicates that the developed countries exported more sharing surplus of exports above their imports whereas the developing economies and the central planned economies imported more than exported. In fact, the countries in Near East have exported about one-third of their imports, accounting for adverse terms of trade for these countries. The trade-deficits are estimated to be the highest on the part of these countries in relation to other regions in the world.

From Table - XIII it is observed that the growth trend of exports from the developed countries is upward from 1978 to 1980 whereas corresponding figure for their imports shows downward. On the contrary, in respect of most of the developing countries the growth trend of the exports is declining during 1978 and 1980 as against its rise in respect of the imports.

In terms of value of imports and exports of the world food trade, imports and exports match each other though there are regional variations. (Table—XIV) For instance, developed market economies' imports increased by more than 3½ times in between 1970 and 1980 whereas their exports rose more than five fold. The imports of the developing market economies increased by more than seven and a half times in 1980 as compared to 1970 ; while their exports went up by more than four times in between 1970 and 1980. The comparative figures of imports and exports of the developed market economies and the developing market economies indicate that the former has favourable terms of trade whereas the latter unfavourable. The adverse terms of trade were still more adverse in respect of the centrally planned economies. For instance, the indices of imports of these countries in 1970 and 1980 were 109 and 888 respectively as against the indice of their exports being (3 and 250 in 1970 and 1980 respectively. The index number of imports of the North America went up from 104 in 1970 to 294 in 1980 whereas the index of its exports rose sharply from 105 in 1970 to 660 in 1980. In conclusion, it may be said that the imports of all the developing economies of the world witnessed the rise in their imports markedly higher than their exports in between 1970 and 1980.

TABLE—XIV

World Trade In Food Products (Exclusive of Fish), 1970-1980 (Value Indices & Trends 1969-71=100)

IMPORTS

	1970	1971	1972	1973	1974	1975	1976	1977	1978	1979	1980	1981
World	100	111	130	187	254	285	274	295	343	408	484	496
Developed Market Economies	100	112	130	182	232	248	239	261	300	348	378	358
North America	104	105	120	150	215	193	189	196	221	259	278	294
West Europe	98	113	133	182	222	248	241	270	314	362	392	352
Oceania	106	109	119	137	263	343	273	313	373	381	430	440
Other Developed Economies	102	115	133	216	310	333	307	308	331	402	445	488
Developing Market Economies	98	112	120	189	315	356	323	352	423	500	691	759
Africa	99	118	130	188	307	375	320	388	468	541	719	788
Latin America	99	107	127	199	323	304	302	316	396	470	705	715
Near East	92	134	130	188	450	561	479	560	671	824	1182	1355
Far East	101	101	105	184	249	284	265	259	299	345	434	489
Other Developing Economies	101	111	135	169	215	239	229	254	299	369	406	431

Centrally Planned Economies	109	108	143	221	285	388	400	404	469	621	774	888
Asian CPE	116	96	138	231	387	275	229	359	398	460	663	701
East Europe and U.S.S.R.	106	112	144	217	253	424	463	419	492	640	810	947
Developed All Economies	100	112	132	186	234	267	263	278	321	380	425	422
Developing All Economies	101	110	122	194	323	346	312	353	420	508	688	752

Source: F.A.O. Trade Year Book, 1981, Vol. 35, pp. 34 & 36.

TABLE—XIV

World Trade In Food Products (Exclusive of Fish), 1970-1980 (Value Indices & Trends 1969-71=100).

EXPORTS

	1970	1971	1972	1973	1974	1975	1976	1977	1978	1979	1980	1981
World	100	111	131	195	258	280	273	297	343	405	482	493
Developed Market Economies	101	115	140	216	268	300	299	313	379	451	554	568
North America	105	115	138	264	337	350	351	338	418	495	605	660
West Europe	99	115	141	198	237	280	281	316	387	463	553	540
Oceania	101	116	145	180	223	259	254	262	272	323	454	479
Other Developed Economies	99	114	127	143	200	244	182	191	229	264	388	388
Developing Market Economies	102	105	120	163	253	266	254	298	318	371	466	428
Africa	105	97	111	137	194	186	186	221	249	264	270	208
Latin America	104	107	127	181	271	303	277	323	341	397	450	437
Near East	93	98	129	173	186	178	221	252	303	324	379	448
Far East	98	114	115	155	311	313	305	357	358	463	536	587
Other Developing Economies	97	97	82	99	228	244	195	257	294	400	394	304

Centrally Planned Economies	93	105	112	157	215	208	184	202	205	240	260	250
Asian CPE	93	104	119	184	278	283	221	193	231	263	313	293
East Europe+	93	105	110	149	194	183	173	205	195	233	248	236
U.S.S.R.												
Developed All Economies	100	114	136	208	259	286	283	300	357	425	517	528
Developing All Economies	101	105	120	165	255	268	251	289	311	362	407	417

Source: F.A.O. Trade Year Book, 1981, Vol. 35, pp. 34 & 36.

India[59] : Value, Composition and Trends of Agricultural Exports and Imports

In respect of exports and imports of India between 1975 and 1980, it is observed that the total value of imports of agricultural products forming 16 per cent of the value of its total merchandise trade declined in 1980 accounting for 7 per cent of the value of its total merchandise trade. Further, the value of imports of India was reduced in 1980 in relation to 1970. Again it is gratifying to note that the value of its total exports increased by almost one and a half times in 1980 as compared to 1970. Especially in the case of food and animals their value of imports declined by more than five times in 1980 in relation to 1970, whereas the value of exports of such items went up by about one and a half times in 1980 as compared to 1970. (See Tables—XVI & XVII for details).

Of the total imports of agricultural products in the year 1975, food and animals formed above 90 per cent followed by forest products and agricultural requisites being 4.8 per cent and 4.6 per cent respectively. But in 1980, agricultural requisites amounted to above 90 per cent of the total agricultural imports followed by animal fats and vegetable oils accounting for 6.9 per cent and food and animals amounting to 2.3 per cent. Thus, in India there has been considerable shift in imports from food and animals in 1975 to agricultural requisites in 1980 indicating that Indian agriculture has shown more tendency of being modernised and mechanised in recent times.

From the point of exports of India, it is found that of the total exports of agricultural products in 1975, the exports of food and animals formed as much as 77 per cent followed by crude materials accounting for above 10 per cent. Beverages and tobacco amounted to 5.8 per cent and more or less the same percentage works out for the exports of fish and fish products. In 1980, the exports of food and animals had declined a little bit forming 75 per cent of the total agricultural exports in 1980 as compared to corresponding

59. Source : F.A.O. Trade Year Book, 1981, Vol. 35, p. 342.

TABLE—XVI

Value and Trends of Agricultural Imports of India, 1970 & 1980, (000 $)

	1975	1976	1977	1978	1979	1980
Total Merchandise Trade	6414505	5732361	6693569	7955000	10143000	14086000
Agricultural Products :	1764321	1679770	1422525	1206242	968639	1322260
Total	(100)	(100)				(100)
Food & Animals :	1646070	1462453	378526	325433	343063	328223
	(90.4)					(2.3)
Beverages+Tobacco :	1244	876	1447	966	644	1687
Crude Materials :	93231	130857	334682	161852	126131	75780
Animal Fats &	23776	85582	707870	717991	498801	916570
Vegetable Oil :	(0.2)					(6.9)
Fish & Fishery Products :	1447	256	368	477	664	700
Forest Products :	84042	74652	116482	116482	182115	182115
	(4.8%)					(1.3)
Agricultural	820431	223717	324044	489885	554100	1235810
Requisities :	(4.6%)					(90.2)

N.B. : Figures in parentheses indicate percentages.

Source : F.A.O, Trade Year Book 1981, Vol. 35, p. 342.

TABLE—XVII

Value and Trends of Agricultural Exports of India 1970-1980, (000 $)

	1975	1976	1977	1978	1979	1980
Total Merchandise Trade.	4418086	5572712	6118988	6415000	6995685	8337000
Agricultural products : Total	1675765	1728003	1916046	1765611	2200302	2408171
	(100)					(100)
Food & Animals :	1300848	1263580	1560562	1402568	1693199	1840283
	(77.2)					(75.00)
Beverages+Tobacco :	124810	110341	137850	137958	140348	162789
	(5.8)					(4.2)
Crude Materials :	211404	303181	183385	174617	279604	329399
	(10.0)					(12.0)
Animal Fats & Vegetable Oil	38703	50901	34247	50468	87151	75700
Fish+Fish Products :	132879	192600	197230	248178	311277	268589
	(5.9)					(8.0)
Forest Products :	22686	31622	28971	28971	26558	26558
Agricultural Requisites :	4504	4476	4829	7985	6799	8780

N.B. : Figures in parentheses indicate percentages.

Source : F.A.O. Trade Year Book 1981, Vol. 35, p. 342.

percentage in 1975. However, the exports of crude materials and fish and fish products had improved in 1980 being 12 per cent and 8 per cent respectively. The position of the exports of beverages and tobacco has been reduced (4.2 per cent) in 1980 as compared to 1975 (5.8 per cent).

In short, relationship between agricultural commodities and industrial manufactures is quite obvious even through international trade. Through manufactured goods and products have been gaining more ground in relation to the 144 agricultural products in the total world trade, international trade in agricultural commodities is increasing in the case of Third World inclusive of India and proves to be one of the important influencing phenomena regarding development of such countries.

7

Sectoral Balance Through Environmental Sustenance

Actions and interactions in agriculture and industry do have bearing on environment. Along with developmental benefits of agriculture and industry, there happen to be environmental hazards. Any policy of development need not therefore neglect such hazards which directly and indirectly are likely to serve as limitations of growth in the long-run. For instance indiscriminate depletion of natural resources through desertification, salinization, silting, soil erosion, deforestation etc. serves as growth-retarding force. Industrial effluents in the rivers and streams cause water pollution. Heavy concentration of industries breed air pollution. Excessive establishment of chemical industries causes toxic-pollutants. Acid rain makes living of the people and animals miserable. Defective educational system gives rise to educated unemployment and social stresses and strains. Half-hearted implementation of family-planning methods make millions of women weak and withhold them from full-time participation in different occupations and other activities. These and other host of environmental considerations are bound to put severe bonds and bondages on the developmental and planning efforts. The developing economies such as India cannot afford such casualties that would prove to be beyond repair after some time. It is likely that the repairing or correctional measures cost in future more than the developmental expenditure. In view of limited resources of the developing countries, wisdom lies in gearing the developmental programmes and projects to the environmental sustenance and ecological balances. It is gratifying that the Seventh Five Year Plan of India has pronounced that any development measure has to be commensurate with the maintenance and continuance of environmental purification and ecological carrying-capacity. Dr. V.K.R.V. Rao[60] has therefore come out with clear understanding of and specific proposal of the need for "balance between agriculture, industry, environment and the quality of life in sustainable development", at the time of his inaugural address to The World Economic Congress, held at New Delhi on 1st December, 1986.

Since environmental reactions and interactions are closely and invariably linked with overall development of any country and with living of people in general, let us have detailed analysis of this problematic issue. Environmentalism though of recent origin of two decades past has clinched a focal attention of both developed and developing countries. Environmentalism is a very complex phenomenon but it needs a unified attack on its pollution.

This has been very vividly expressed by American President Richard M. Nixon at the time of reorganisation of federal environmental responsibilities of Environmental Protection Agency in 1970. "Despite its complexity, for pollution purposes the environment must be perceived as a single inter-related system. A single source may pollute the air with smoke and chemicals, the land with solid wastes, and a river or lake with chemical and other wastes. Control of air pollution may produce more solid wastes, which then would pollute the land or water ......A far more effective approach to pollution control would

---

60. Indian Economic Journal, October-December 1986, Vol. 34 No. 2. p. 12,

indentify pollutions, trace them through the entire ecological chain, observing and recording charges in form as they occur determine the total exposure of man and his environment examine interactions among forms of pollution ; and indentify where on the ecological chain interdiction would be most appropriate"[61]. Environmental pollution and environmental purification are two facets of the same complex phenomenon. Pollution arises from both development and under-development. Underdevelopment breeding poverty gives rise to ill-health, malnutrition, slums, misery, etc. The poverty-alleviation measures undertaken by most of the under-developed countries are remedies to such evils. What remains to be done for pollution emanating from development process itself is a big problem. To start with different types and extent of pollution are to be studied and later purification measures would be examined.

The Expert Committee Report at the United Nations Conference on the Human Environment convened at Founex, Switzerland in June 1971 has grouped environmental side effects into a number of categories as following :

(i) Resource deterioration (the deterioration, for example, of minerals, soil or forest resources).

(ii) Biological pollution (the pollution represented by agents of human disease and by animal and plant pests.

(iii) Chemical pollution (arising out of air pollution, industrial effluents, pesticides, metal, detergent components and similar agents)

(iv) Physical disruption, as reflected by thermal pollution sitting and noise, for example.

(v) Social disruption, of which congestion and a loss of a sense of community are examples.

Further, Report of the Meeting of a Working Party[62]

---

61. The American Review, Vol. 30 No. pp. 3—4, 1-1986, cited in the article "Balancing The Risks" by William D. Ruckelshaus.

62. ADC Bulletin—Teaching Forum : Development Processes and Planning, No. 27, January 1973.

convened by SCOPE at Canberra, Australia between 24 August and 3 September 1971 has summarized the environmental problems in the developing countries. In this context environmental hazards have been enumerated as below. —

Uncontrolled increase of urban population ;
increases in the number and variety of endemic and epidemic pathogens and pests ;
exhaustion of natural resources ;
continuation of traditional land-use practices which prevent the accommodation of higher population pressures ;
degradation of the environment stemming from wide spread use of chemicals that are alien to natural processes.

From above mentioned both reports, it is quite evident that there are different types of pullution and different kinds of environmental hazards. To illustrate some of such hazards and pollutions, certain examples are worth mentioning. Maggie Suzuki has cited a number of such instances relating to some South-East Asian countries.[63] He states"......most of South-East Asia's rainforests have already been degraded and destroyed by a combination of logging and conversion to desperately poor agricultural land by squatters following logging roads into the forest......It is impossible to estimate just how much forest land has been wasted, but one indication is that the Philippines, which was virtually 100 percent forested 50 years ago, now counts only 11 per cent of its area as forested, with a shocking 42 per cent classified as 'marginal land', waste land left after deforestation". The consequences of tropical deforestation reach beyond the tragic direct destruction of species. One far reaching result is disruption of water cycle. All forests act like sponges to soak up and slowly release water, a function very important in rain-forests where at least 4000 mm of rainfalls annually (4 times as much as in New York city), often in heavy downpours. Rainfalling

63. IPPF Reviews of Population and Development, "People" Vol. 13, No. 4, 1986 (Earth Watch Japan pp. 7—8 Number *26, 1986).*

on deforested land runs off instead of sinking in, causing great difficulties for people living and farming irrigated rice down stream. Increased erosion and siltation clogs canals and dams, deforestation upstream of the Ambuklao Dam in the Philippines has caused so much siltation in the reservoir that the useful life of the dam has been halved. So far as India is concerned, the eco-destruction of the Himalayas as revealed by the Satellite data, protends a grace threat to the environmental stability of the entire Indian subcontinent. The forest cover in the Himalayas which was estimated to be 60 per cent at the turn of the century has been reduced to around 12 per cent. The mountain slopes once covered with green forests now bear only weeds and other unwanted vegetation.[64]

Overfishing has destroyed the resonaletage and decreased the yields. Another threat to fisheries is pollution. More than 40 rivers in the Philippines and 42 rivers in Malayasia have been declared dying from pollution. Experts agree that oil spills, chemical wastes and heavy metals dumped into rivers and seas are the most serious forms of pollution and require urgent action to limit damage. Pollution of Europe's coastal waters and rivers is steadily growing. Hardly a day goes by without an oil spill or chemical leak posing a new treat to marine life.[65]

Dr. S. Dillon Ripley[66], an eminent environmentalist, from Smithsoman Institute said at a seminar in Delhi that in India "massive exposure of land, the soil and water and the air to the fruits of technological advance and development without regard for essential biological precepts can only hasten the degradation of what has been a fair land and a marvellous one for all manner of life". Firm evidence of this came through the well-documented World Conservation Strategy prepared by the International Union For Conservation of Nature and

64. Ecological Ruin of Himalayas by Radhakirshna Rao, Sunday Herald February 22, 1987, Bangalore.
65. EUROMAR vs Marine Pollution by Nikolaus Mess Deccan Herald Bangalore, June 25, 1987.
66. Competition Master, December 1986. p. 348,

and Natural Resources in cooperation with the United Nations Environment Programme and the World Wildlife Fund. This revealed that more than half of India suffers from some form of soil degradation. Out of a total of 3.3 million sq rg. km, 1.4 million is subject to increased soil loss, while an additional 2,70,000 sq. rg. km is being degraded by floods, salinity and alkalinity. An estimated 6000 million tonnes of top soil and six million tonnes of plant nutrients are lost every year.

Water conservation is also a world wide problem[67]. It is estimated that the world wide demand for water is rising at an annual rate of six per cent. Since the water stock is constant, there arises a genuine fear that, before the end of the century "the wells will run dry". It need not be except perhaps in arid and semi-arid regions. Since world population expands at barely two per cent a year, it is evident that the increasing demand for water stems much more from prosperity industrialization and unrbanization than from the demographic explosion.

Subsidence of the land in some areas and landslides in the hilly tracts are problems affecting highways, human life habitations and irrigation dams. The contributions which the nutrients lost through water erosion make, to the degradation of surface water supplies are considerable. It has resulted in greater algal growth in lakes, ponds and other water bodies and is the first-step of entrophication of a body of water. The organic matter and sediment load contribute to entrophication and shorten the life of reservoirs and make the treatment of water for domestic use more costly. It has been stated that the life of most of our dams has been considerably reduced due to alluvial deposits. It has also been estimated that loss of nutrients, particularly nitrates and phosphates by soil erosion is the major factor of water pollution which some ecologists unwittingly ascribed to the fertilizers. An idea of the loss of nutrients through erosion can be had from the table on the following page.

67. "Water Conservation—A World wide problem", Intellect, June 1978. pp. 473-477,

Loss of Nutrients Through Soil Erosion

	8% slope kg/ha	0.5% slope kg/ha
Organic matter	2167.7	86.8
N_2	228.1	5.8
P_2O_2 (available)	70.5	10.7
K_2O (available)	28.8	4.28
Ca	382.7	53.4
Mgl	103.3	41.4

Source : Yojana, June 1—15, 1987, Vol. 31, No. 10, p. 6, "Agriculture versus Environment" by R. Gopalkrishnan.

Technology which had seemed to be a boon to the world is a kind of paradox. It provides many of the things which improve the quality of life, but in some cases it is responsible for lowering the quality of an environment. Irrigation is a blessing when it makes the arid lands productive but it becomes a course when it results in making the soil saline and alkaline. Likewise fertilizers and pesticides are most important factors for increasing agricultural production and feeding increasing population, but their continuous use particularly of the pesticides is fraught with danger. Under pressure of population which is increasing in an exponential manner, man is forced to use the land more extensively as well as intensively and employ more and more technology and industrial inputs which is not an unmixed blessing, as numerous problems of land degradation also begin to appear. Modern agricultural being input-intensive and technology-intensive, the effect of these on the soil has become a matter of concern and a anxity to the man.[68]

Founex Committee Report has glaringly pointed out how traditional agriculture, modern agriculture and River Basin

68. For details, please see of articles in Indian Journal of Agricultural Economics (Conference Number), July-September 1987, Vol. XLII, No. 3-"Impact of Agricultural Development on Ecology & Environment."

Development have been causing environmental pollution. Traditional agriculture in many tropical regions is characterized, particularly under stress of expansion, by a range of environmental hazards. These include leaching-notably the rapid leaching of nutrients and degradation of planned farmland following the removal of a forest; rapid soil depletion resulting from permanent cultivation which the relative infertility of the soil cannot support without the addition of nutrients, soil erosion the rough variable and heavy rain falls and prolonged droughts or flash floods, and indiscriminate loss of forest resources through slash-and-burn techniques.

Even the welcome emergence of the high yielding varieties of wheat, rice, maize and other cereals can sometimes give rise to certain negative side effects, both because these varieties require larger quantities of chemicals such as pesticides and also since they replace hardy native species which by natural selection, are often better suited to the adversities of local conditions and are valuable for inter-breeding. Again constant tillage which is facilitated by mechanization can also damage soil structure.

Some of the environmental problems which are generally associated with the river basin devleopment projects include the spawning of water-borne diseases, the filling of reservoirs with sedimentation, the drying-up of down-stream fisheries, the spread of salination and water-logging in associated irrigation projects, the innundation of valuable agricultural and forestry land, the displacement of population and the loss of mineral resources, wild life areas or valuable historical sites.[69]

Chemical pollution has been making human life increasingly miserable. Minamita tragedy, the tragedy of the inhabitants of the Love Canal near Niagara falls. New York, 'Itai-itai' disease and "Yusho" disease which have affected a large number

---

69. Op. cit, A/D.C/ Bulletin, No. 27 January 1973.

of people in Japan are the instances. Acid rain which contains 65 per cent of sulphuric acid, 30 per cent nitric acid and 5 per cent hydro-chloric acid is caused by pollutants which fossil-fuel-based industries emit. It has destroyed considerable vegetation. Sweden and Canada are the worst victims of acid rain which is no respector of national boundaries. The growth of chemical industry has been as incautious as it has been rapid. The extent of the problem can be gauged from the fact that from about 40 to 50 known industrial pollutants around the 1940s and early 1950s, there are now about 30,000 toxic chemicals entering the environment in massive amounts as a direct result of human ingenuity. Public anxiety has been aroused by the spate of recent industrial accidents involving chemical factories in Goa, Bombay and Delhi, with the Bhopal disaster setting the record as the worst industrial disaster in world. This anxiety is further heightened by recent investigations into industrial safety. The Committee headed by Dr.R.K. Garga, Head of the Department of Chemical Engineering Division of the Bhabha Atomic Research Centre reported "only seven per cent of the chemical factories are safe".[70]

Air pollution including gaseous leakage of chemical pollutants, acid rain, thermal pollution, nuclear explosives in the air, smoke and smog let loose through factory chimneys, etc. is another threat to human life. Surveys have revealed that India has suffered greater havoc by destruction of natural wealth and pollution of the environment than other countries. India as a whole is adding about 4 million tonnes of sulphuric dioxide, 7 million tonnes of particulates, one million tonnes of carbon monoxide, besides nitrogen oxide, hydrocarbons and several other toxic substances. Bombay illustrates the catastrophic dimensions of air pollution in the country; with all its industries, it emits daily 1000 to 1700 tonnes of pollutants. In Calcutta about 1300 tonnes of pollutants are discharged every day. Because of the three thermal power stations and massive burning of domestic fuel, Delhi has suspended parti-

---

70. "Toxifying Our Planet'; by Averthanus L.D' Souza. Sunday Herald, Feb. 22, 1987 p. 3.

culate matter as high as 640-1000 micro-gram per cubic metre one of the highest in the world. Delhi is a topper in respiratory diseases, the other badly affected towns are Kanpur, Ahmedabad and Coimbatore.[71]

As elsewhere in the world, especially the U.S.A., Britain West Germany and Japan, pollution by automobile emissions poses a great danger to the environment in India—greater than damage done by industries. The increasing number of motor vehicles in the country, the exhaust emissions (especially of diesel run trucks), poor maintenance of roads, the increasing firewood consumption pollute the air in urban areas.

The rapid pace of environmental destruction in India through soil erosion, deforestation, pollution and urban decay is already affecting the lives of million of poor people; the country faces social, economic and ecological disaster if its environment is not properly managed.[72] The report seeks to establish a link between environmental destruction in rural areas and urban decay. Many slum and pavement dwellers in India's cities are "ecological refugees".

Assessment of Hazards and Risks

Beefore discussing the measures to have environmental purification, it is necessary to study source of the attempts already made to assess the hazards and risks that accompany environmental pollution. At a 1987 conference of the International Institute of Applied Systems Analysis (HASA) in Vienna, representatives from 20 global modelling groups made presentations. Donella H. Meadows has summarized the attempts made by these models to assess the environmental risks and hazards in her article "Global Models" published in the American Review, Vol. 3) No. 1,-1/1986. The broad features of such models and their findings are worth noting. The methods and philosophies of global modellers are so diverse

71. Competition Master, December 1986, p. 348.
72. The Second Citizen's Report on the State of India's Environment 1984-85, November 1985, released by the New Delhi based Centre for Science and Environment (CSE); Quoted in Ibid, p. 349.

that one would hesitate to call the models a single body of intellectual work, except that they are directed toward the some intertwined problems: population growth, poverty, resource scarcity, environmental deterioration and international instability. Another point of commonality is that many of the models were made in response to the ones that came before. Collectively the global models constitute a fascinating international debate. They reveal the world's knowledge, uncertainty and opinion about global problems. Given the different starting points, the debate about global issues is leading to a surprising convergence of opinion. In fact, global models are not meant to predict, do not include every possible aspect of the world, and do not support either pure optimism or pure pessimism, about the future. They represent mathematically assumptions about the interrelationships among global concerns such as population industrial output, natural resources and pollution. Global modellers investigate what might happen if policy,continue along present lines or if specific changes are instituted.

The first global model "TheLimits To Growth" was developped by a team headedby DennisMeadows of MIT at the behest of Club of Rome in 1970. The model looked into five major trends of global concern, namely, (a) accelerating industrialization (b) rapid population growth, (c) wide-spread malnutrition, (d) depletion of non-renewable resources, and (e) a deteriorating environment. These trends are all inter-connected in many ways and their development is measured in decades and centuries. Further, it has come to the following conclusions:

1. If the persent growth trends continue, the limits to growth on this planet will be reached within the next one hundred years. The probable result is decline in population and industrial capacity.

2. It is possible to reverse these trends provided basic material needs of each person on earth are satisfied, each person has equal opportunity to realize his individual human potential.

3. If the world's people decide to strive for this second outcome rather than the first, the sooner they begin working to attain it, the greater will be their chances of success.

These findings have been arrived are on the basis of following assumptions:

(a) Population will be slowed down only by increased industrialization. (b) The model assumes a constant level of industrial and agricultural productivity. (c) Physical capital determines amount of production. (d) Land is fixed in supply. (e) Natural resources are also fixed in supply. (f) Pollution increases in proportion to an increase of agricultural and industrial output.

Of course, these assumptions are criticised and a noted Pakistani economist Mahabub Hal Haque has argued that the basic weakness of the 'Limits To Growth' is not so much that it is alarmist but it is complacent..... about the social and political problems which its own prescriptions would only exacerbate.[73] Regarding population, increased industrialization in developing economies appears to be costly and time consuming. Meanwhile, it is fall in death rates that decreases birth rates. In respect of constancy of productivity, historical development in the past 200 years do not support and hance, technological development need not be neglected. Total amount of production is determined by social capital and human capital other than physical capital. Discovery of synthetic substitutes, availability of more land in LDCs and depletion of productivity will upset the assumption of fixed supply of land. New resources such as hydroelectric power, nuclear power, petroleum and aluminium etc. nullify the assumption of fixed natural resources. As regards pollution new capital pollutes less than old capital and technology now exists to eliminate pollution at low cost. The possible solution to the income distribution conflict i.e. negative growth in the developed countries and positive growth in the developing countries,

---

73. Cited in "Economic Development—An Introduction" by Clarence Zuvekas, 1979, pp. 389-392.

massive migration from the developing countries to the developed ones or a world income tax would not be easily agreed to by the developed countries, which are now reluctant to transfer one per cent of a rising GNP to the developing world.[74] The model itself is a very broad one and did not distinguish among different regions of the world.

Mihaijlo Mesarovic at Case Western Reserve University in Cleveland, Ohio and Eduard Pestel at The Technical University in Hannover, West Germany designed the World Integrated Model (WIM) to explore the same questions with more regional detail. These scientists reached similar conclusions except that their warnings were expressed in even more urgent and dire language.

The Latin American World Model of the Funda Cion Bariloche in Argentina is constructed atround an explicit value i.e. meeting basic human needs. According to that model the world could work well with that priority. Latin America and Africa could meet the basic needs of their entire population through their own efforts by the year 2000. Asia would take longer and require outside aid. The rich countries would not collapse or even stagnate, and as human needs were met everywhere, the population would stabilize. The modellers appeal that less developed countries need not follow the pattern of industrialized societies. Even if it were possible, it is not desirable, as it would mean to follow the same road which led to the present situation of wasteful and irrational consumption, accelerated social deterioration and increasing allevation.

The Model of International Relations in Agriculture (MOIRA) built by a coalition of agronomists from Wagningen University in the Netherlands and economists from the Free University, Amsterdam represents food production, consumption and trade for 106 nations. In spite of sufficient food in the world, hunger persists. The reasons behind this paradox lie in uneven distribution of national income and twisting of

74. Ibid.

food surpluses in the developed countries for their own benefit, and not for the benefit of less developed countries. As such, the model suggests changes in resource distribution for the benefit of the poor and keeping exports and imports of the rich countries regular and constant for stabilizing world prices.

The Global 2000 model built by the U.S. Council on Environmental Quality to study global prospects for the year 2000 came out with gloomy findings for the future. It warns that if the present trends continue, the Land World be ecologically less stable and more valnerable to disruption than the world we live in now. Earth will be more precarious in 2000 than it is now, unless the nations of the world act decisively to alter current trends.

Certain common conclusions from these global models are mentioned here:

1. Existing resources and known technologies can support all the needs of the world's people today and for some time to come.
2. Population and physical capital cannot grow for ever on a finite planet.
3. No reliable, complete information is available about the degree to which the Earth's environment can absorb the wastes created to meet human needs.
4. Present world policies will lead to an increasing gap between rich and poor.
5. Technology can help but is not an answer.
6. The interdependence among peoples and nations is much greater than commonly imagined.
7. Policy changes made soon are likely to have more impact with less effort than the some changes made later.
8. Many amplex international programmes and agreements are based on inconsistent assumptions.

From the above discussion it is true that global models have been intellectual excercises in giving some information about broad trends of the world forces. The solutions to the complex problems have to be worked out by the individual countries to keep the globe beautiful and dear.

Measures of Environmental Purification

All world authorities recognise that unless the man learns to use the limited natural resources, of soil and water, he will face serious crisis. What the world needs more, is the efficient use of these resources for maximising agricultural production per unit area and per unit of time without the impairment of the environment. Man should care to maintain an optimum relationship between economic production and ecological stability.[75] State gives developed to increase agricultural production must work with nature and not against it. We must discard these practices which lead us to commit ecological aggression against our environment. The modern seeds are only the catalysts and the main break-through in agricultural production is to came through better management of soil and water. Man will need, above all, to learn to view his world in a holistic, integrated way—for the simple reason that the world is an integrated interdependent system. This integration supplies the basic principle or natural law of ecology, a law that can—with only minor exaggearation—be stated: "Everything affects everything else".

For the last two decades at least, the importance of measures to purify environmental pollution has gained momentum both in developed and underdeveloped countries. In America, to start with, Environmental Protection Agency (EPA) has been established as for back as 1970. Subsequent passing of Clean Air Act and Clean Water Act has enabled the U.S.A. to control pollution and to ensure at an increasing rate purification of environment. "The United States has made significant progress in many, if not all, environmental areas where laws

75. Yojana, June 1-15, 1987, p. 5.

and institutions have been explicitly devised to address specific problems. Most of the conventional air pollutants no longer pose a health threat to nearby communities; the majority of rivers are suitable for fishing and swimming; exposure to some specific toxic substances—lead, PCBS, chlorinated hydro carbon pesticides—has declined: the populations of many wild life species are increasing."[76] However, the direct transfer to developing countries of knowledge and technologies generated in industrialized countries is seldom successful because of ecological, cultural and socic-economic differences. This is especially true in the domain of management of national resources, but it is also true in the case of introduction of new industries. What is needed is new techniques that are ecologically oriented to local needs. To this end, national and regional knowledge-generating centres should be created (or strengthened if they exist) and charged with the responsibility of finding biologically sound solutions to environmental problems.

From the foregoing analysis of different aspects of environment, environmental relationships and assessment of the environmental hazards, the following areas appear to be of major concern to developing countries.[77]

(a) the development and management of natural resources,

(b) the improvement of human settlements,

(c) the control of pollutional and environmental hazards,

(d) educations and

(e) institutional arrangements for solution of environmental problems.

(a) Development and Management of Natural Resources

Maintenance of natural resources in keeping with quality of human life is prerequisite for management of natural resources. It depends on (1) "carrying capacity of environment" which varies according to the plant and animal species

76 American Review. 1/1986 quotation of William K. Reillu, President, Conservation Foundation, p. 5.

77. ADC Bulletin No. 27, January 1973.

of the area and also in relation to the socio-economic values of the society, and (2) information and knowledge of the people to adapt with and manage ecosystems. The natural resources management therefore has to take the following into consideration: (1) Development plans and policies have to include a diversity of projects and cater for alternate projects even at the planning stages. This is to safeguard against the hazards of monoculture and dependence on a single product or highly limited range of products. (2) In the process of development, certain areas representing the principal natural ecosystems need to be reserved for continual monitoring so that the functioning of natural systems can be compared with man-made replacements. This will have the added value of maintaining sources of biological diversity and of providing sites that can be used for education or outdoor recreational purposes. (3) Social, cultural and historical factors have to be considered a part of the ecosystem in the formulation of development plans.

To fill basic gaps of information about soil, water, mineral, plant and animal resources, surveys and inventives are needed in most of the developing countries. The are to be associated with research programmes associated with identification and functioning of ecosystems. Multinational programme of research are also needed. There has to be a two-way flow of information between the research workers and, the planners and decision makers, so that all relevant knowledge will be utilized in the process of decision-making.

With specific reference to Indian agriculture and environment Dr.R. Gopalkrishnan opines "Agriculture is the only known method for the production of food and therefore it has to be necessarily practised the existence of man. But man has to be careful to see that the techniques and practices that he adopts should not upset the natural processes and impair the life-supporting system in nature."[78] Similarly, A. Ram Reddy highlights the hazards of deforestation in his article

78. Yojana, June 1-15, 1987, p. 18.

"Tackling Deforestation On Warfooting" and suggests the measures as following.[79] Forest operations are labour-intensive. Nearly 80 per cent of the expenditure is in the form of wages to labourers, thus afforestation provides a great relief to the rural unemployed people. The most challenging task before us today is afforestation taking village as a unit. The greater emphasis should be on those villages which have already been devastated by ecological imbalances. The local people in these areas join at their will in massive afforestation schemes as they are feeling that deforestation is a war at their door-steps. In other regions for agroforestry and other forms of social forestry, not aimed only at commercial forestry, be taken up at rapid pace simultaneously educating them about the consequences of deforestation. The government should also bring an act of systematic grazing. The menace of large-scale denudation of the forests by the forest contractors and other officials can be reduced by strict vigilance and by providing alternatives to wood in the costruction of buildings, agricultural tools furniture, etc. Whatever may be the reasons the burning of cow dung and fuel wood is not replaced by bio-gas and other non-conventional energy resources at an expected rate. Planting specific trees according to the needs of industrial emissions around the industrial infrastructural areas and creating a green belt should be strictly implemented to check the pollution.

Professor Dhirendrakumar Dixit draws attention on various pest devils and calls for integrated approach to the war against insects and pests including both biological control, evolving pest resistance crops and introducing genetically modified pests into natural populations. "In the ultimate analysis, in the context of the global shortage of food and the recurrence of diseases, the war against insects and pests has to be intensified. The farmers and public health authorities need to adopt an integrated approach to pest management, utilizing a variety of control technologies in an economically and ecologically sound fashion. An integrated

79. Ibid, p. 10.

approach must include the use of chemicals that interfere specifically with the bio-chemical systems of the pest but do not harm the environment, the use of biological control agents and natural products, evolving pest-resistant crops, and the introduction of genetically modified pests into natural populations; adjusting planting time and use of a combination of seeds, each resistant to different pests; and finally improved formulations and application methods of pesticidal chemicals. Multipronged attack, on a warfooting is the need of the hour and the time to act is now or never."[80]

Shifting cultivation in North-Eastern India is considered to be a destructive practice. Through that facility of the soil exhausts rapidly and its capacity to retain plant nutrients becomes low and farmers clear the forest for sake of attaining more fertile patch of land. To overcome shifting cultivation, the ICAR model of multi-disciplinary nature has been advocated by M.P. Jagirdar of NIRD, Hyderbad. The model comprises (a) agriculture on the lower hillside with bench terraces, (b) horticulture in the middle portion of the hills with half-moon terraces and contour bunds, and (c) agro-forestry on the hill-top with contour bunds. The model envisages the bench terraces and contour bunds as conservation base, which can provide stable alternative for shifting cultivation without much disturbing their life-style. Though the model involves intensive farming with precise scientific methods, an honest attempt by the developmental agencies through trial and error method will definitely yield promising results.[81]

In short, to avoid depletion and deterioration of natural resources, soil conservation measures, afforestation, water resources management, horticultural development, agricultural planning, stoppage of fire-wood consumption as fuel and prohibition of overgrazing, careful use of pesticides and other chemicals in agricultural practices are to be pursued on urgent and intensive lines.

---

80. Ibid, p. 13.

81. Ibid, p. 23.

(b) **Improvement of Human Settlements :**

In less developed countries such as India, human settlement has become quite complex and expensive. Most of the cities grew bigger just because of flow of people from rural areas and they were not planned. As it is, the villages are not planned. Industries also developed in an unplanned manner. The consequences are over—croowding, poor sanitation and adverse social conditions. Town planning authorities and municipalities have been struggling very hard to keep the cities clean. Similarly, local governments are trying to make villages liveable. In planning process, lot of attention is being given to the rural development and efforts are increasing to make them urbane. Still, the task is gigantic and costly. The problems are multiplying. However, to minimize adverse effects developing countries have to adopt the following measures in rigorous manner :

1. National policies on population planning,
2. careful siting of new industries to avoid over concentration of population,
3. improvement of the facilities in rural areas (for example, opportunities for education and for training integrated agricultural practices).
5. Efforts to preserve a sense of community among groups that have moved from rural to urban areas.

(c) **Pollution Control**

Major source of pollution in the urban areas is concentration of industries and unsystematic and unplanned industrial growth. Secondly, haphazard transport development. Thirdly, there is no sufficient space for public parks, playgrounds, zoo, etc. New industrial colonies and extension of cities are nothing but slum areas. To stop these evils, industrial licensing to be brisk asking the investors to make provision for anti-pollutants along with their establishments. The vehicles need to be devised in such a way as not to cause noise and smok emission. The roads and railways also need to be developed in proportion to the carrying capacity of the cities. Master-plans for every village and city are to be framed and hygienic and systematic development has to be insisted and followed up the governments to beautify and cleanse the sourroundings.

(d) Education

In the developing economies, there is a need of reforming education in such a manner that at all levels of education environment content of the syllabus forms an indispensable component. Teachers' knowledge has to be refashioned on environmental importance and instruction. Researchers and scientists have to engage themselves to a large extent how to maintain and increase environmental carrying capacity of the nations. Newspapers, radio and television have to give effective coverage to events of environmental importance. Seminars and short-term courses also need to be organised involving scientists, decision makers as well as executives for stimulating awareness of the importance of environmental purification. Extension workers and village level workers have to be trained on these lines so as to help guiding the villagers and other illiterate people in keeping their surroundings clean and beautiful. Nevertheless, the following suggestions are worth noting in this connection :

1. Creation of cooperative links among institutions dealing with similar problems.
2. Exchange of scientific personnel and students among developing countries and between developing and industrialized countries.
3. Establishment of regional and inter-regional training courses.
4. Organisation of seminars and advanced short courses with the participation of scientists from industrialized countries.
5. Financial support and scientific assistance from national and international agencies.

(e) Industrial and Legislative Arrangements

Of course, to put an end to all sorts of environmental hazards, many countries in the world are quite afoot in passing necessary legislations and establishing a number of institutions devoted for solving the problems of pollution. There are several international organisations committed to such programmes.

SUOPE Working Committee came out with relevant observations as far back as 1971 and they are worth reproducing here for the benefit of readers and policy makers. There is increasing recognition among the scientific community that an interdisciplinary approach is necessary for the solution of environmental problems. Institutional arrangements should concentrate on :

1. Identifying environmental problems that need immediate solution and promoting research to solve them,
2. coordinating the activities of the different institutions involved in research on environmental problems,
3. promoting the training of research workers and scientific personnel at all levels,
4. obtaining funds to support environmental research and training,
5. serving as a liaison body between the scientists and the decision makers within and outside the country.

It is increasingly evident that other environmental problems of global nature (such as pending climatic changes and ocean pollution (can best be solved through international cooperation. Growing fear of fundamental damage to human cells imperilling both present and future generation led to the formation of Environmental Mutagens Societies, first in the U.S.A. in 1969 and subsequently in Europe and Japan. The Environmental Mutagen Society of India was founded in 1974 by a small group of concerned scientists and has now grown into a national association of genetic toxicologists. On the initiative of the International Association of Environmental Mutagen Societies, the International Commission for Protection against Environmental Mutagens and Carcinogens was formed in 1977. Enventually the International Programme on chemical Safety (IPCS) was created in 1980 as a cooperative global venture of the U.N. Environment Programme (UNEP), the ILO and WHO. The main objectives of this IPCS are : to carry out and disseminate evaluations of the risk to human health from exposure to chemicals based on existing information and data ; to encourage the use and improvement, and in some cases, the validation, of methods for laboratory testing and epidemiological studies that are suitable for health evaluations ; and propose appropriate methods for assessing health risks, hazards, benefits and exposure; to promote effective international cooperation with respect to emergencies and accidents involving chemicals ; and to promote training of the manpower needed for testing and evaluating the health effects of chemicals and for the regulating and other control of chemical hazards. Mr. Averthanus D 'Souza concludes his article on 'Toxifying our planet' by saying "The Toxification of our planet through uncontrolled chemicalisation is posing a danger that is as great as, if not greater than, the threat posed by the building up of nuclear arsenals. While the threat of nuclear destruction is of a cataclysmic nature, the chemical threat is as grave, only the manner of destruction is slowly corrosive and more subtle.......Time for action is Now. Tomorrow may be too late".[82]

Since the Stock Golun Session there have been U.N. Habitat Conference on Human Settlements in Vancouver in 1975 and the U.N. Desertification Conference in Nairobi in 1977 and the latest international conference on the question of saving trees and forests in January 1986 at Paris. In India in particular, Water Pollution Preventation Act of 1974 and Air Prevention and Control of Pollution Act of 1980 were in operation. But both Acts were proved to be of more recommendatory than implementability. However, recently in 1986 the new Environmental Protection Act has been passed and put into practice with more stringent provisions.

82. Sunday Herald, Bangalore, February 22, 1987, P. 300.

Seventh Plan Strategy on Eco-Development

The Seventh Five Year Plan of India has come out with specific environmental purification measures and programmes. Every development project/ programme has to be carried out commensurate with environmental sustainable capacity of the nation. A total outlay of Rs. 427.91 crore has been allocated for this programme during 1985-90. Of this, Rs. 350 crore is in the central sector, Rs. 75.71 crores in the State sector and Rs. 2.20 crore in the Union territory sector. Out of 350 crore in central sector, Rs. 240 crore has been earmarked for the Ganga Action Plan. The Seventh Five Year Plan strategy on environmental goals relates to :

—Institutionalising the process of integrating environmental management and development.

—Inducing organisations at the central, state and local levels to incorporate environmental safeguards in their plans and programmes.

—Establishing a strong science and technology base for environmental research and development, demonstration and extension activities.

—Strengthening mechanism for ensuring mechanism for corrective action with regard to environmental degradations that have already taken place.

—Creative awareness among the people for effective environmental management by utilising existing institutional framework and seeking full cooperation of more than 200 non-governmental organisations or voluntary agencies working in the field.

The government of India is also in contact and collaboration with a number of international agencies to combat this huge problem. The plan document of the Seventh Plan has further appealed to the mass-participation for eco-development. It visualises that the problems encountered in the field of environment in India arise due to conditions of poverty and underdevelopment as also the negative effects of development programmes which have been badly planned or badly implemented

The whole planning process is aimed at development and the removal of poverty. The need to improve the conditions of our people is pressing ; under this pressure many concerned with developmental activities lose sight of environmental and ecological imperatives.

Realisation concerning these aspects has been with us for only a relatively short period of time, about a decade and a half. The damage being done to the environment, because of the large size of the population and its increase, and the scale of developmental activities, is of such magnitude, says the document, that urgent remedial measures are called for. Official and voluntary agencies must work together to create the needed awareness ; indeed, environment is all-pervasive, and the success of our efforts in this area will ultimately call for the involvement of the entire population at all levels. This, says the document, is a philosophy which must permeate the entire effort in the field of environment.

8

Conclusion

It is observed in the foregoing chapters that rate of growth of agricultural sector in terms of production rate participation in world trade, employment opportunities, sectoral investment, human factor, institutional growth etc., is not on par with the rate of growth of non-agricultural sector. In order to pull up agricultural growth in developing economies production policies need to be reoriented so as to absorb increasingly a modern technology and to make small farmers more accessible to production resources and services. Secondly, there is a need to change the existing institutions in agriculture and to create new institutions suitable for rapid development in agriculture. "Stagnation and growth with inequality in the rural economies of the contemporary developing Asia can be attributed, in substantial degree, to the prevalence of inappropriate institutions that are characterised by high degree of inequality in the distribution of land and assets".[83] Thirdly, the developing countries need to make efforts of creating non-farm employment opportunities for the redundant labour prevalent in rural areas especially in agricultural sector. "It must be noticed that off-farm employment alone cannot guarantee the sustained economic development of rural areas.

83. Growth & Equity In Agricultural Development, Proceedings of Eighteenth International Conference of Agricultural Economists 1983, p. 236.

Agricultural productivity has to be raised in order to have balanced development. Productivity increase in agriculture not only increases the demand for industrial inputs but also releases more labour hours to be utilized in off-farm activities. In sum, off-farm employment should be integrated with overall rural development efforts. Growth of off-farm activities in rural areas depends not only on government efforts to relocate non-farm industries but also on the steady growth of agricultural productivity".[84] Fourthly the world agricultural growth is to be conceived basically in terms of accelerating the rate of growth of production in developing countries. "This is in the mutual interests of both the developed and developing countries. It would help correct the growing imbalances in world trade caused by rising food imports of developing countries. Furthermore, world agricultural growth would contribute to overall world economic growth".[85]

Keeping these considerations in view, it is thought that there is no other better way than quoting the findings of the study[86] made by F.A.O. in respect of "Agriculture Toward 2000 : The Long Term Perspectives of contemporary Issues In World Food & Agriculture". A purpose of the study was to provide governments and the United Nations with quantified perspectives of world and country group demand for, and production and trade of food and agricultural commodities, including implications for such areas as nutrition, investment, assistance, and research. Pre-publication results of the study were the major source for the food and agricultural component of the UN International Development Strategy (IDS) adopted in 1980. A second purpose was to provide FAO, its member governments, and other qualified users with a detailed quantification on a common pattern of possible

84. Ibid, p. 377.
85. Ibid, p. 211.
86. Rural Development—Growth & Inquiry—IAAE Occasional Paper No. 3, edited by Bruce L. Greenshields and Margot A. Bellamy (This paper presents the main feature of a recent study by FAO, hereafter referred to as AT 2000).

alternative paths of change in agricultural sector of 90 individual developing countries.

At 2000 is an analysis of the agricultural sector of the entire world, with the exception of China, to the year 2000. The focus is mainly on assessing the requirements and potential for improvements of food and agricultural section of the developing countries.

All the analyses are conducted country by country for 90 developing countries (accounting for 98 per cent of the population of the developing countries excluding China) and all 34 developed countries. Production prospects for the developing countries are analysed in greater detail than for developed countries.

The analysis covers 28 crop and 6 livestock commodities or commodity groups. It starts with exogenous growth rates of population and total GDP as inputs into detailed projections of food demand. Projections of non-food industrial demand are added to make up projected total final demand. Two intermediate demand categories (breed and seed) and an allowance for post-harvest waste are project jointly with production.

The next step in the analysis is to set for developing countries a vector of preliminary production targets by commodity which, together with the vector of final domestic demand, is entered into a model which internally calculates the feed, seed, and waste components, and draws up balancing equations for each commodity of production, total domestic demand, and net trade (Supply Utilization Accounts or SUAs). Production targets are defined in the first instance in terms of desired levels of self-sufficiency for the deficit commodities, and desired levels of exports for the exportable commodities. From this phase onwards, the core of the analysis concerned with : (1) testing establishing, after iterative revisions, the feasibility of the production targets ; and (2) ensuring international compatibility of the trade balances of the individual countries.

Policies and Strategies [87]

The world framework of agriculture will probably not change fundamentally between now and 2000 except that the pressure on parts of the sector would mount severely. The major concern in world food and agriculture is therefore undoubtedly to help extricate the low income countries from the trap of low production, low consumption, and rapidly increasing dependence on outside food supplies.

The AT 2000 study concludes that this objective could be generally met, although only if the broader goal GDP growth around 7.0 percent per year is also attained. Low income countries must participate fully in the growth process. No economically or politically feasible alternative exists to the necessity for the great bulk of the approximate doubling in food demand in the developing countries between 1980 and 2000 being met from their own production, chiefly by increasing yield (includind multiple cropping). The implication is one with which agricultural economists are familiar a steady transformation is required of traditional farming methods (which have usually been oriented basically to security of yields) into higher yielding technologies. This change is already coming about but is limited in speed and extent.

There is no quick solution, What is evident, however, is the need to shift completely away from earlier models of national development in which policy priority went to industry, with energy and armaments also coming to the fore recently while agriculture was considered a sector with low capital requirements capable of supplying funds and an increasing surplus of food for the rest of the economy without much attention. By quantifying in detail, country by country, the physical requirements for better agricultural performance, AT 2000 underlines the need for more balanced policies. Most developing countries therefore need to review very critically their policies bearing on food and agriculture so as to improve incentives to and supplies of production requisites for farmers

87. Ibid, pp. 273-275.

and to enlarge the flow of credit and investment funds. In many developing countries, sustained production growth (and the need for adequate growth in demand to sustain output expansion) will require increasing the access of small farmers to production resources and services.

The role of research and extension will be vital in the modernization of agriculture in developing country. While basic research must continue into various aspects of tropical and arid zone agriculture (notably as to how continuous mechanized farming can be carried on in tropical zones with fragile soils the greatest need is for adaptive research which can pay off fairly quickly. Those planning long term research programmes should recall that about 80 per cent of the increase to 2000 in world demand (excluding China) for agricultural products will come from developing countries. At present, at least that share of world research expenditure is made in developed countries, primarily for the b enefit of their own agriculture. Results of expanded research must also be brought to farmer. The estimate of a four-and-a-half-fold increase in trained field level extension workers between 1980 and 2000 simply to provide one for about every 500 farmers in irrigated farming and one for every 1 ,000 farmers in rainfed farming underlines the magnitude of the expansion required in the capacity of training institutes.

At 2000 is neutral as regards prices which enter the models only for deriving aggregates. The whole thrust of the supply-demand analysis, however, points to the need to improve incentives to producers in the majority of developing countries. This will require modification of the common policy in which controlled prices favour urban populations. But incentives are a broad package, and the study advocates more attention to assurance of future prices, of raising the actual return to the farmer through improved marketing, and as noted, to considerably greater access to credit and other services. Increasing requirements of manufactured inputs to farm production must be available. Efficiency and stability in the administration of the country cannot be quantified, but are clearly of the first importance to agriculture. For instance, in every developing country which suffered civil war or other serious internal disorder during the last one or two decades, agricultural production growth was temporarily checked and often fell in absolute quantities.

The scenario results point to the continuation of widespread and serious undernutrition. The frequent question of whether production or distribution presents the more important policy issue is unhelpful. The two are intimately interrelated; at any one time there is need and great scope for nutritional improvements through better distribution of income and access to income earning assets, while over the longer run the imperative of good production growth is the dominating influence.

Policy must, however, turn to ways of improving the purchasing power or the food producing capacity of the poor if serious undernutrition is to be reduced sharply. Economic growth alone, even at high rates, would take far too long. Policy makers must therefore explore the full range of possible measures ranging from substantial land reform to subsidized food for selected groups of economically vulnerable people. Where lage scale land redistribution is not politically realistic, policy must turn to more limited measures to rural labour productivity and to protect the cosumption levels of low income urban populations.

The third set of policy implications is international. World agricultural trade would continue to rise under any of the scenarios, and developed countries would enjoy expanding markets for cereals and livestock products. To enable developing exporters also to expand sales of products which could be provided in greater volume (such as sugar, vegetable oils, and citrus) protection would have to be reduced in developed countries. USSR and Eastern European consumption of imported tropical products is low. Since growth in developed country farm output (at the 34 country group level) cannot at best be higher than in the past, and would need to be lowered under scenario. A outcome for developing countries, present structural adjustment problems being experienced by developed countries would continue.

The real issue of future food imports of developing countries is not one of the physical capacity of exporters to generate supplies, but rather one of institutional and financial arrangements. In the end, much will depend on the developing countries' capability to pay for increased imports, and this is not independent of international policies affecting their capacity to earn foreign exchange. If production in low income countries remained at trend levels, their cereal import requirements would rise fourfold. The future arrangements for concessional cereal imports could therefore have substantial implications for the ability of low income countries to improve diets through increased imports.

External assistance to agriculture is another international issue raised by the scenario findings. At 2000 emphasize the heavy investments in agriculture implied by modernising production. Despite misgivings often expressed as to the effectiveness of some aid, it is difficult to see how low income developing countries could meet the heavy investment needs of agriculture which AT 2000 points to without additional help. The study proposes that cid pronide approximately 1 dollar in 6 of their investment expenditure in primary agriculture.

In sum, while most to the world should continue to experience acceptable, (although not trouble-free) conditions in food and agriculture, dismal prospects for a large minority of poor countries and poor people from a continuation of long term trends imply the need for some radical reorientation of national and international policies.

From the above generality illustrated in accordance with the observations as mentioned in the "Proceedings of Eighteenth International Conference of Agricultural Economists 1983" relating to Growth and Equity in Agricultural Development, particular policies pertaining to Indian case can very well be cited in the words of Professor V.K.R.V. Rao as following:

......[88] I wonder what special importance can be attached to the question of balance between agriculture and industry in development. I am not denying the linkages, forward and backward, between industry and agriculture in economic development. Agriculture in its producer aspect meets the needs of industry in respect of both food for its workers and raw materials for its products. Agriculture, as producer-consumer, provides a market for the industrial production of agricultural inputs like fertilisers, tractors and tillers, and steel and cement for building dams, reservoirs, and canals, also for lining the canals, with the plastic industry now stepping in as a substitute, and also for the new system of sprinkler irrigation. Agriculture as consumer needs the basic mass and, hopefully, also the conventional consumption goods required by its population that are produced by Industry. The vast numbers of our agricultural population constitute an immense potential market undisturbed by quotas and tariffs; but to realise this potential into an actual mass market, agricultural incomes will have to increase, not only of small cultivators, and medium and big farmers but also for the labourers they hire in cultivation; and this means higher prices for agricultural produce and higher wages for agricultural workers. It also means high investment, both public and private, not only to make land more productive but also for post harvest operations such as storage, inland transport, and marketing. Increase of the purchasing power of the rural masses must also include the marginal cultivators who are under-employed and the rural non-agricultural workers who have lost their markets to the products of modern urban industrialization and now swell the ranks of the rural unemployed. All this means increased resource mobilisation on the one hand and higher cost of living for the urban population and non-agricultural workers in the rural region on the other. Unless industrial employment is taken into the rural areas and there is decentralisation in the industrial development process, there

88. Indian Economic Journal, Vol. 34, No. 2, "Balance Between Agriculture And Industry In Economic Development" by V.K.R.V.Rao, pp. 11-12.

can be no substantial decline in the percentage of the labour force now employed in agriculture and other traditional rural occupations; and if this is not done, there can be no reduction in the existing disparity between the per capita income in the rural sector and that in the urban sector or in the per capita product of rural and urban economic activity. The balance one needs between Industry and Agriculture in development must necessarily involve both a dispersal of industrial activity and its decentralisation, along with markets additional to or even exclusive of local markets and dependence on local materials. Also a third variable has to be brought into the development process basides Industry and Agriculture namely, the environment. For sustained and sustainable development, one needs a balance not only beetween agriculture and industry in terms of mutual exchange and markets but also in terms of the economic processes involved in both agriculture and industry not adversely affecting the environment and disturbing, if not actually destroying, the ecological balance. And this balance between agriculture, industry and environment need not, indeed, should not, be confined within national boundaries but must cross them, increase international trade, and permit the harnessing of comparative advantages in costs and supply of natural resources. Natural resources are not evenly distributed by national boundaries, nor is the environment and the help it can give, and the harm it can do, confined within national frontiers. The environment is both local and world wide; and only a global attitude and its implementation in policies and programmes can protect the environment and ensure human harmony with Nature to the mutual advantage of both in terms of sustenance and further development. The balance between agriculture and industry has to be global and equitable in its operations not only across national boundaries but also within them. The balance between economic growth, which includes all the three sectors of the GDP, and the environment which covers them all, has not only to be implemented across national frontiers but also within them. Development cannot be left without a qualifying adjective which will take it out of the short period and from purely personal or group selfish interests into the broader field of the long period and harmonisation of the personal and the social interest; and it must deal with the quality of life rather than merely with material goods and needs. Science must be combined with spirituality.

Appendices

APPENDIX A
TABLE-I

Country	%Share of Services in GDP, 1984	Per Capita GNP, 1984 (in U.S.A.)
1. Canada	72	13,280
2. Denmark	70	11,170
3. U.S.A.	66	15,390
4. Netherlands	64	9,520
5. France	62	9,760
6. U.K.	62	8,570
7. New Zealand	60	7,730
8. Japan	56	10,630
9. Brazil	52	1,720
10. Mexico	52	2,040
11. Federal Republic of Germany	52	11,130
12. Argentina	50	2,230
13. Kenya	48	310
14. Pakistan	47	380
15. South Korea	47	2,110
16. Malaysia	44	1,980
17. Nigeria	43	730
18. Yugoslavia	40	2,120
19. Bangladesh	39	130
20. India	38	260
21. Indonesia	34	540
22. Poland	33	2,100

Source: The Indian Economic Journal, October- December, 1986, p. 13.

APPENDIX B

TABLE-II

Country	Per Capita GDP in 1984-	Percentage Share in GDP of		
		Industry	Agriculture	Services
1. U.S.A.	15,390	32	2	66
2. Canada	13,280	24	3	72
3. Denmark	11,170	25	5	70
4. Federal Republic of Germany	11,130	46	2	52
5. Japan	10,630	41	3	56
6. France	9,760	34	4	42
7. Netherlands	9,520	32	4	64
8. U.K.	8,570	36	2	62
9. New Zealand	7,730	32	9	60
10. Argentina	2,230	39	12	50
11. Yugoslavia	2,120	46	15	40
12. South Korea	2,110	40	14	47
13. Poland	2,100	52	15	33
14. Mexico	2,040	40	9	52
15. Malaysia	1,980	35	21	44
16. Brazil	1,720	35	13	52
17. Nigeria	730	30	27	43
13. Indonesia	540	40	26	34
19. Pakistan	380	29	24	47
20. Kenya	310	21	31	48
21. India	260	57	35	38
22. Tanzania	210	31	33	—
23. Bangladesh	130	12	48	38

Source: ibid, p. 14.

APPENDIX C

TABLE-III

Country	%Share of Labour Force in Industry		%Share of Industry in GDP		Per Capita Income(in US$)	
	1960	1980	1960	1981	1960	1981
1. Federal Republic of Germany	48	44	53	46		13,450
2. U.K.	48	38	43	33		9,110
3. Netherlands	42	32	44	33		11,790
4. France	39	35	39	35		12,190
5. Denmark	37	32	39	32		13,120
6. U.S.A.	36	31	38	34		12,820
7. Argentina	36	24	38	38		2,560
8. Canada	35	29	34	32		11,400
9. Japan	30	34	42	43		10,080
10. Yugoslavia	23	33	45	43		2,790
11. Mexico	20	29	29	37		2,250
12. Pakistan	18	16	16	266		350
13. Brazil	15	27	35	34		2,220
14. Malaysia	12	19	18	36		1,840
15. India	11	13	20	26		260
16. Nigeria	10	12	11	37		870
17. Zaire	9	13	27	24		210
18, South Korea	9	27	19	39		1,700
19. Indonesia	8	13	14	42		530
20. Kenya	5	7	18	21		420
21. Tanzania	4	5	11	15		280
22. Bangladesh	3	6	8	14		140

Source: ibid, p. 15.

APPENDIX D

TABLE-IV

	Country	% Share of Labour force in agricuture		% Share of Agriculture in GDP		Per Capita Income (in US $)
		1960	1980	1960	1980	1960 1981
1.	Tanzania	89	86	57	52	280
2.	Bangladesh	87	75	61	54	140
3.	Kenya	86	81	38	32	420
4.	Zaire	83	72	30	32	210
5.	Indonesia	75	57	54	24	530
6.	India	73	70	50	37	260
7.	Nigeria	71	68	63	23	870
8.	South Korea	66	36	40	17	1,700
9.	Yugoslavia	64	32	24	12	2,790
10.	Malaysia	63	42	37	23	1,840
11.	Pakistan	61	55	46	30	350
12.	Mexico	55	37	16	8	2,250
13.	Brazil	52	31	10	13	2,220
14.	Japan	33	11	13	4	10,080
15.	France	22	9	10	4	12,190
16.	Argentina	20	13	17	9	2,560
17.	Denmark	18	7	14	4	13,120
18.	Federal Republic of Germany	14	6	6	2	13,450
19.	Canada	13	5	6	4	11,400
20.	Netherlands	11	6	9	4	11,790
21.	Australia	10	7	12	5	11,080
22.	U.S.A.	7	4	4	3	12,820
23.	U.K.	4	3	4	2	9,110

Source : ibid, p. 16.

APPENDIX E

TABLE-V

Country	% Share of Labour Force in Services 1960	1980	% Share of Services in GDP 1960	1981	Per Capita Income (in US $) 1960	1981
1. U.S.A.	57	66	58	63	12,820	
2. Canada	52	66	60	64	11,400	
3. United Kingdom	48	56	53	65	9,110	
4. Netherlands	47	49	47	63	11,790	
5. Denmark	45	58	47	64	13,120	
6. Argentina	44	59	45	53	2,560	
7. France	39	53	51	61	12,190	
8. Federal Republic of Germany	38	50	41	49	13,450	
9. Japan	37	49	45	53	19,080	
10. Brazil	33	46	49	53	2,220	
11. Mexico	25	39	55	55	2,250	
12. Malaysia	25	34	45	41	1,840	
13. South Korea	25	37	41	44	1,700	
14. Pakistan	21	23	38	44	350	
15. Nigeria	19	27	26	40	870	
16. Indonesia	17	30	32	34	530	
17. India	16	18	30	37	260	
18. Yugoslavia	13	36	31	45	2,790	
19. Bangladesh	10	15	31	32	140	
20. Kenya	9	12	44	47	420	
21. Zaire	8	12	43	44	210	
22. Tanzania	7	11	32	33	280	

Source : ibid, p. 17.

Bibliography

Adam Smith : An Inquiry Into The Causes of Wealth of Nations.

Adelman, Irma : Theories of Economic Growth And Development.

Agarwala, A.N. & Singh S.P. : The Economics of Under-development.

Agarwala, S.N. : Indian Population Problems.

Alex, A.V. : Human Capital Approach to Economic Development

Anderson, C.A. & Bowmen, Mary J. (ed) : Education & Economic Development.

Amlan Dutta (ed) : Paths to Growth.

Amlan Dutta : Perspectives of Economic Development.

Amartya Sen (ed) : Economics of Growth.

Balough : Economics of Poverty.

Barlogh, T. : Some Aspects of Economic Growth of Under-developed Areas.

Barnett, H.J. : Scarcity and Growth.

Baldwin, R.E. : Economic Development & Export Growth.

Baur, P.T. : Dissent on Development.

Bertain, H. : Under-development & Development—The Third World Today.

Bicanic, R. : Problems of Planning--East & West.

Bicanic, R. : Turning Points In Economic Development.

Boner : Theories of Population.

Bos, H.C. : Towards Balanced International Growth.

Bos, D.S. : Public Enterprise Economics.

Baster, Nancy (ed) : Measuring Economic Development.

Barrie, W.D. : The Growth & Control of World Population.

Barkley, P.W. and Seckler David : Economic Growth And Environmental Decay.

Bognar, J. : Economic Policy & Planning in Developing Countries.

Brahmananda, P.R. : Failing Economy and How To Revive It.

Buffa : Modern Production Management.

Byers, T.J. (ed) : Foreign Resources and Economic Development.

Cairncross, A.K : Factors in Economic Development.

Chopra, K.R. : Dualism and Investment Pattern.

Colin Clark : Conditions of Economic Progress.

Colin Clark : Transforming Traditional Agriculture.

Coole & Hoover : Population Growth and Economic Development.

Cornehis, J.V. : Economic Growth & Economic Development in Under-developed Countries.

Cooper Charles (ed) : Science, Technology & Development.

Clerk Kerr & Paul D, Staudohar (ed) : Industrial Relations in New Age.

Colman, David & Nixon, Frederick. : Economics of Change in Less-Developed Countries.

Cassen, R : Does Aid Work.

Casse Robert & Wolfson Margaret (ed) : Planning For Growing Populations.

Chaubey, N.O. : Motivational Dimensions of Rural Development.

Chondhun Pramit : The Indian Economy—Poverty & Development.

Coverlabe, G.M. : Planning Education in Relation To Rural Development.

Dallan, George : Economic Development And Social Change.

Dobb, M. : Capitalism, Development & Planning.

Dutt, Ratna & Joshi, P.C. : Studies in Asian Social Development.

Dutt, James : Taxation and Economic Development in India.

Dwivedi, D.N. : Economic Concentration And Poverty in India.

Dandekar and Rath : Poverty of India.

Datta, Bhabatosh : Economics of Industrialization.

Dhar and Lydall : The Role of Small Enterprise in Indian Economy.

Dalton, G. : Economic Development and Social Change.

Ezekiel, Hannan : Industry

Ellsworth Economics of International Trade.

E.A.G. Robinson & Michael Kidron : Economic Development In South Asia.

Eicher & Witt : Agriculture In Economic Development.

F.A.O. : World Agriculture.

F.A.O. : Provisions of Indicative World Plan For Agricultural Development.

Fillol, T.R. : Social Factors in Economic Development.

Friedmann J. : Regional Development Policy.

Friedman, Irving S : Inflation—A World-Wide Disaster.

F.A.O. : Trade Year Book, 1981, Vol. 35.

Fransman, Martin : Technology & Economic Development.

Fiege, Edgar L. (ed) : Underground Economics.

GATT : International Trade.

Galbraith : The New Industrial State.

Ghosh Alak : Indian Economy—Its Nature & Problems.

Ghosh Alak : The Changing Profile of India's Industrial Policy,

Ghatak, S. : Introduction to Development Economics.

Gross Bertram : Action Under Planning : The Guidance of Economic Development.

Gove Hambidge : Dynamics of Development.

Ginsberg, Eli, Noylle T.J. & Stanback (Jr) T.M. Technology And Employment (concepts & clarifications)

Hahen, F.H. : Readings in Theory of Economic Growth.

Haq Mahabub Ul : The Poverty Curtain.

Higgins, B. : Economic Development.

Hirsch Fred & Goldthrope John	: The Political Economy of Inflation.
Hams, S.E.	: Economic Planning.
Harrod Roy	: Policy Against Inflation.
Hirschman, A.O.	: Strategy of Economic Development.
Hicks, Ursula & Others	: Federalism And Economic Growth In Underdeveloped Countries.
Hagen, E.	: On the Theory of Social Change.
Hanson	: Process of Planning.
Haswell, M.R.	: The Economics of Development : Village India.
Hoselitz, B.F.	: Sociological Aspects of Economic Growth.
Hansen, B.	: Long and Short-term Planning In Underdeveloped Countries.
Hanberg, D.	: Models of Economic Growth.
Hartwell R.M.	: Industrial Revolution and Economic Growth.
Hiestand, D.L.	: Economic Growth & Employment Opportunities.
Hodder, B.W.	: Economic Development in Tropics.
Hughes, D.J.	: Science & Starvation—Introduction to Economic Development.
Holis Chenery & Others	: Redistribution With Growth.
Harbinson, Frederick and Myers, Charles. A.	: Education, Manpower And Economic Growth.
IBRD	: Population Policies & Economic Development.
Ignacy Such (Translated by Peter Fawcett)	: Development & Planning.

I.L.O. : Recent Developments In Certain Aspects of Indian Economy.

Inagaki, M. : Optimal Economic Growth (Shifting Finite versus Infinite Time Horizon).

Jarret, H. : Environmental Quality in A Growing Economy.

Jaubauskas, E.B. : Human Resources Development.

Jacob, N. : Modernisation Without Development.

Jacoby, E.H. : Agrarian Reconstruction.

Jefferson, R. : Planning and The Innovation Progress.

Jha, L.K. : Economic Strategy For The 80s.

Jha, L.K. : Economic Development : Ends & Means.

Jha Prem Shankar : A Political Economy of Stagnation.

Jones, R.V. (ed) : International Trade : Survey of Theory & Policy.

Johnston : Economic Development & Structural Change.

Kamark, A.M. : Economics of African Development.

Kindleberger, E.P. : Economic Development (2nd edition).

Kuznets, Simon : Economic Growth.

Kassalow, E.M. : Role of Social Security in Economic Development.

Kool, R. : Tropical Agriculture & Economic Development.

Katzenstein, Peter (ed) : Between Power & Plenty : Foreign Economic Policies of Advanced Industrial States.

Keith Griffin (ed) : Institutional Reform and Economic Development in The Chinese Countryside.

Kabra : The Black Money In India.

Khusro, A.M. : Economics of Land Reform and Farm size In India.

Krugman, Paul R (ed) : Strategic Trade Policy And The New International Economics.

Lewis, Arthur : The Theory of Economic Growth.

Locklin, D.P. : Economics of Transportation.

Loehr, William & Powelson, John P : Economics of Development & Distribution.

Leibenstein, Harvey : Economic Backwardness & Economic Growth.

Lewis, J.P. : Quiet Crisis In India.

Lipton, Michael (ed) : Fertilizer & Economic Development.

Levitan, S.A. : Human Resources & Labour Markets.

Lincoln, Julian Simon : Theory of Population and Economic Growth.

Marshall, Alfred : Principles of Economics.

Mamoria, C.B. : India's Population Problems.

Mancur Olson : The Rise And Decline of Nations.

Meier, G.M. & Baldwin : Economic Development.

Mellor, John, W : The Economics of Agricultural Development.

Meier, G.M. : Leading Issues In Economic Development.

Meier, G.M. : International Economics Of Development.

Morgan, Betz & Choudhary : Readings In Economic Development.

Mountjoy Alan B. (ed) : Developing The Underdeveloped Countries.

Mac Bean, A.I. : Export Instability And Economic Development.

Meade, E. : Planning & Price Mechanism.

Mishan, E.J. : Growth : The Price We Pay.

Meade, E. : Growing Economy.

MeQeen, M. : The Economics of Development Problems & Policies.

Myint Hla : The Economics of The Developing Countries.

Minami, Ryoshin : The Economic Development of Japan.

Myrdal, Gunnar : Asian Drama.

Myrdal, Gunnar : Theory of Underdeveloped Regions.

Myrdal, Gunnar : International Economy,

Misra, R.P. : Regional Development Planning In India—A New Strategy.

Meyer, C.H. : Staff Development In Public Welfare Agencies.

Murray, D. Bryce : Industrial Development.

Nag, D.S. : Problems of The Under developed Economy.

Nanavati & Anjaria : Indian Rural Problem.

Nader Claire & Zahlan, A.B. : Science & Technology In Developing Countries—(IE Conference at Beirut, 1967).

Nurkse, Ragnar : Problems of Capital Formation In Underdeveloped Countries.

North D.L. : The Economics of Public Issues.

Nickson, J.W. : Economics & Social Choice.

Nassef, E.S. : Monetary Policy In Developing Countries.

Naomi Caiden & Asran Wilda Vasky : Planning & Budgeting In Poor Countries.

New World Order Series : Ashis Publishing House
Vol. I—Economic Theory & New World Order.
Vol. II—International Commodity Policy.
Vol. III—Technology Transfer by Multinationals.
Vol. IV—New Protectionism And Restructuring.
Vol. V—Resource Transfer & Debt Trap.
Vol. VI—Challenge of South—South Cooperation.

Ogg, F. A. : Economic Development of Modern Europe.

Okun and Richardson : Studies In Economic Development.

Overbeck, J : History of Population Studies.

Owens, Edgar and Shaw Robert : Development Reconsidered.

OECD : Choice & Adoption of Technology In Developing Countries

" : Economic & Political Considerations And Flow of Financial Resources To Developing Countries.

" : Employment Problems In Less developed Countries.

" : Fiscal Policy And Employment Problem In Developing Countries.

" : Government Finance & Economic Development.

" : Multidisciplinary Aspects of Regional Development.

" : Population Programmes & Economic & Social Development.

" : Public Finance as an Instrument For Economic Development.

" : Social Change & Economic Growth.

" : Technical Assistance And The Needs of Developing Countries.

„ : Energy & Environment.

Pandey, M.P. : The Impact of Irrigation on Rural Development.

Pitchford, J.D. : Population In Economic Growth.

Powelson, J.P. : Institutions of Economic Growth.

Papanek, F. Gastow (ed) : Development Policy—Theory & Practice.

Perrings, Charles : Economy and Environment.

Poole, R.E. : Public Finance & Economic Welfare.

Pusic, E. : Planning The Social Services In Developing Countries.

Proceedings of Eighteenth International Conference of Agricultural Economists, 1983.

Raj, K.N. : Indian Economic Growth—Performance & Prospects.

Ranade, M.G. : Essays In Indian Economics.

Reynolds, Lloyd, G : Agriculture in Development Theory.

Rangarayan C, *et al* : Strategy For Industrial Development in The '80s.

Ranis, Gustov : The Gap Between Rich And Poor Nations.

Rao, Hanumanth & Joshi. P.C. (ed) : Reflections on Economic Development And Social Change (Essays In Honour of V.K.R.V. Rao).

Rao, V.K.R.V. (ed) : Essays In Economic Development.

Rangnekar, D.K. : Poverty And Capital Development In India.

Ray, Jefferson : Progress in Planning Vol. 3-Planning & Innovation Process.

Ray Rajat K : Industrialisation of India—Private Corporate Sector.

Ray, S.K. : Economics Of Black Market.

Ray, S.K. : Indian Economy.

Ray, S.K. : Economics of The Third World.

Raymond, A Pathorpe (ed) : People Planning & Development Studies.

Robson, W.A. : Nationalised Industry And Public Ownership.

Robinson, E.A.G. (ed) : Problems In Economic Development.

Rostow, W.W. : The Process of Economic Growth.

" " : The Economics of Take-off Into Self-Sustained Growth.

" " : Why The Poor Get Richer And The Rich Slow Down.

Robbins, L. : The Theory of Economic Development In the History of Economic Growth.

Robert, B.B. : Financing of Economic Development.

Ronald Robinson, : Developing The Third World.

Rees, W. : Crisis of World Inflation—The Reigning Error.

Rowbey C.D. : The Politics of Educational Planning In Developing Countries.

Rante, I. : Aid And Overseas Development.

Rauss, F.G. : Fiscal Policy For Growth Without Inflation—German Experiment.

Richman, B.M. : International Management And Economic Development.

Rielly, J.E. : Development Today.

Rivkin : Area Development For National Growth.

Sachdeva : Economics Of Agriculture.

Saha Panchanan : Immigration of Indian Labour.

Schickele, Rainer : Agricultural Revolution & Economic Progress.

Schemmell, W.M. : International Monetary Policy.

Schurr, S.H. (ed) : Energy, Economic Growth & The Environment.

Schultz, T.W. : The Economic Organisation of Agriculture.

Schultz, T.W. : Economic Growth & Agriculture.

Schaffer, Bernard : Administrative Factors—Papers in Organisation, Politics & Development.

Sen, A.K. : Employment, Technology & Development.

Sen, Amartya (ed) : Economics of Growth.

Sen, Sudhir : Richer Harvest—New Horizons For Developing Countries.

Sen, P.K. : Indian Economic Growth—Constraints & Prospects.

Shannon (ed) : Underdeveloped Areas.

Singer, S.F. : Is There An Optional Level of Population ?

Singer, H.W. : International Development—Growth & Change.

Singh, Charan : India's Economic Policy.

Sinha, V.C. : Dynamics of India's Population Growth.

Sowelem, R.A. : Towards Financial Independence In A Developing Economy.

Streeten & Lipton : The Crisis of Indian Planning.

Streeten, Paul : Unfashionable Economics.

Stewart (ed) : Economic Development And Structural Change.

Stigtiz Joseph E & Uzawa Hirofum (ed) : Readings In The Modern Theory of Economic Growth.

Spangler, M.B. : New Technology & Marine Resource Development.

Spencer, M.H. : Management Economics—Decision Making & Forward Planning.

Staley, Eugene : The Future of Underdeveloped Countries.

Starkee, D. : Transportation Planning & Public Policy.

Snodgrass, M.M. & Wallace, L.T. : Agriculture, Economics & Growth

Scitovaky, Tibor : Progress on Welfare & Growth.

Simpsen, E.S. : The Developing World.

Shroff, Guhan S : Essays on Economic Progress & Welfare (In Honour of I.G. Patel)

Shukla, Tara (ed) : Economics of Underdeveloped Agriculture.

Solomos Solomon : Phases of Economic Growth 1850-1973.

Salvatore, D.R. (ed): The New Protectionist Threat To World Welfare.

Stanford, C.T. : National Economic Planning

Swartz and Bonello: Taking Sides—Clashing Views on Controversial Economic Issues, (2nd edition).

Seymour Broadbridge: Industrial Dualism In Japan.

Southworth & Johnston : Agricultural Growth & Economic Development.

Jabah Leon : Demographic Problem To Development.

Todaro, M.P. : Economics For A Developing World.

Tondon, B.C. : Economic Planning—Theory & Practice.

Tondon, B.C. : Economic Development of Developed Countries.

Taylar, D. : Development Means People.

Tsoukalis, Laukas Europe, America & The World Economy.

Uphoff, Norman T. (ed) : Rural Development & Local Organisation in Asia.

Uppal : Indian Planning.

United Nations Organisation : Measures For Economic Development of Underdeveloped Countries.

" " : Economic Development And planning In Asia And Far East.

" " : Regional Planning.

" " : Hand Book of International Trade And Development Statistics, 1981 Supplement.

" " : Multinational Corporations In World Development.

" " : World Economic Survey 1981-82.

" " : Studies on Development Problems In Selected Countries of The Middle East.

U.S. Congress Joint EconomicCommittee : Monetary Policy, Selective Credit Control And Industrial Policy In France, Britain, West Germany And Sweden, 1981.

Vakil, and Brahmananda : A Grammar of Indian Planning.

" " : Planning For An Expanding Economy.

Van Horne : Financial Management & Policy.

Veblen : Theory of The Leisure Class.

Vittas, Dimitri (ed) : Banking Systems Abroad.

Wan (Jr); Henry Y. : Economic Growth (Theories).

Wall D. : The Third World Challenge—Preferences For Development,

Warriner, Doreen : Land Reform In Principle And Practice.

Wharton : Subsistence Agriculture And Economic Development.

Williamson and Buttrick : Principles And Patterns of Economic Development.

Wilson, T. : Papers on Regional Development.

Wilczynski, J. : Profit, Risk & Incentives Under Socialistic Economic Planning.

Wootton, Barbara : Freedom Under Planning.

" " : Plan or No Plan.

Waren, W. : Inflation And Wages In Under-developed Countries.

World Bank : Working Papers on Agriculture.

" " : World Development Papers 1975 to 1985.

" " : India's Population Policy.

Wykstra : Human Capital Formation And Manpower Development.

Yoshihara, K. : Japanese Economic Development (2nd edition).

Zinkin, M : Development For Free Asia.

Zebot, C.A. : Economics of Competitive Coexistence—Convergence Through Growth.

Zuvekas, Clarence : Economic Development. (Int. College edition)

Zysman, John : Governments, Markets And Growth.

Zweig, Ferdynand : The Planning of Free Societies.

Index